LOOKING TERRIFIC

About the Authors

Emily Cho founded the personal fashion consulting industry in 1970 with her firm, New Image. Her prior professional experience includes work as a Bloomingdale's buyer, fabric editor and fashion show coordinator for *Seventeen,* photography editor and stylist at *Vogue* Patterns, and booking agent for the Ford Model Agency. Ms. Cho lives in New York City.

Linda Grover is currently head writer of the NBC television serial *The Doctors.* She has contributed to *The New York Times, McCall's, Cue,* and the *New York Post,* and is the author of *The Housekeepers.* Ms. Grover also lives in New York City.

LOOKING TERRIFIC

Express yourself through the language of clothing

BY EMILY CHO
AND LINDA GROVER

Illustrations by Catherine Clayton Purnell

BALLANTINE BOOKS · NEW YORK

Copyright © 1978 by Emily Cho and Linda Grover

This edition published by arrangement with G.P. Putnam's Sons, New York

Library of Congress Cataloging in Publication Data

Cho, Emily.
    Looking terrific.
4.6   1. Clothing and dress.   I. Grover, Linda,
joint author.   II. Title.
TT507.C56 1979   391'.07'2   79-15127
ISBN 0-345-28259-0

Manufactured in the United States of America

First Ballantine Books Edition: September 1979
        4   5   6   7   8   9

CONTENTS

PART I

THE
LANGUAGE

Chapter 3   The Fashion Game

What's the Use of Fashion, Anyhow? · Fashion to History · Status: The Primary Clothing Message · Shifting Erogenous Zones in Female Clothing · How and Why Fashion Changes · The Ever-Quickening Pace · The Birth of a New Look · A Rose Between the Teeth and Other Excesses · Planned Obsolescence · Keeping Up with the Times

PART II   Chapter 4   Women's Changing Self-Image

YOU   *Such Shame About Our Bodies · How We've Been Fantasized by Men and the Media · Clothing Has Kept Us in Traditional Roles · Toward a More Honest Expression of Self and Sexuality · "Isn't My Wife Beautiful? Don't Touch!" · We're Expected to Excel in Every Role · The Female Professional · Establishing Rank and Combating Sexual Discrimination · Clothing Can Keep You in a "Safe" Place · Self-Acceptance*

Chapter 5   Finding and Expressing the Inner Self

Clothing Can Do a Lot, It Can't Do Everything · Beginning with the Clothing Image and Working Inward · How to Find Your Personal Style The "Little Waif" Within You · "Look Good, But Don't Spend Time on It" · Stuck in One Period of Our Lives · Stereotyping Ourselves Comments Vs Compliments · Models Aren't Really Beautiful · The Art of Illusion · Vocabulary and Grammar of the Clothing Language The Focal Point · Balance · "What Can I Do About My Age?" Getting Out of a Rut · Try Something New · What Does Color Say About You? · Balancing Color · Traditionalist Vs Trend-Lover One Step at a Time · Try This on for Size

Acknowledgments

To those who served beyond the call of friendship: Doreen Chu, for her initial encouragement and inspiration; Betsey Cohn, Linda Meisner and Sunny Rhodes, for their good advice and counsel; Helga Balaban and Linda Sklaroff, for their invaluable assistance with photography.

To Max Millard, Tina Marsh, Linda O'Brien and Linda Pieper who, with intelligence and enthusiasm, typed, retyped and edited far into the night.

To the clients and friends who lent both themselves and the clothes on their backs so that this book could present real-life examples, and illustrate from truth: Nancy Bate, Gay Vincent-Canal, Jorie Feitelson, Lynn Gilbert, Harriet Griffin, Eva Hartwig, Judy Licht, Lucy Littlefield, Sandra Lowenstein, Bonnie Sacerdote, Audrey Smaltz and Victoria Zoellner.

To Michael, who has more than generously given of his male insight, good judgment, and patience to this book.

And, lastly, to Owen Laster of the William Morris office, and our editor, Diane Matthews, who had faith in this book when it was only an idea.

The Promise

It was one of those lovely, early-fall days in New York, when color seems new and the solemn skyscrapers sparkle in the sunlight. I was on my way to meet a client for a shopping date when my cab stopped for a light at 50th Street and Fifth Avenue. The crowd spilled off the sidewalk and swirled around us—hundreds of people hurrying on their way, and each, through clothing, projecting his or her own special message to the world. Secretaries, perfect in their magazine chic ... Long Island matrons, with fur coats and shopping bags ... a couple from out of town, clutching brightly clad offspring firmly by the hand ... and a small covey of businessmen in assorted shapes and sizes, attired in carefully ranked suits of brown and gray and navy worsteds and flannels. Once again, I realized how important clothing is to our identity.

Modern life is fast. Contacts are brief, and often we get just one chance to tell another human being who we are. We must make an instant statement. We can't afford to waste an opportunity by not sending the right signals, or to make the wrong move because we don't understand another person's message or intention. In business, politics or love, often words are not enough, so we signal both our mood and

There Is a Clothing Language

11

our intent through what we wear. Without the identity clues provided by clothing, we'd find life more difficult and much less interesting.

Clothing language is an important visual code that projects our talents, our needs, our personalities, our dispositions and our destinations. Without a doubt, when we dress, our psyches are showing.

We've all experienced better treatment when we look especially well, and most of us also know what it's like to be treated badly when we don't look so great. People close to us relate to the way we dress, and so do strangers. Our clothing says, "Hey, I feel beautiful," or, "I'm important." "I'm as good as you are, and expect to be treated that way." Or, clothes may reveal, "I'm not so sure about myself," "I'm depressed," "I'm angry," "I'm feeling aggressive." By overlooking the importance of your image and style, you're apt to convey uncertainty, awkwardness or low self-esteem.

By emphasizing the positive aspects of yourself through your dress, you can inspire confidence in your abilities and your judgment; you can make people happy and excited just to be in your presence. In fact, a clear personal style can spark your own inner assurance and can help to enhance your natural beauty, strength and success. Clothing is a self-fulfilling self-portrait. Instead of keeping your inner self a secret, or demonstrating your flaws, you can put your talents and values on the outside, and display them where they will do the most good.

Generally, the powerful and the wealthy understand the importance of communicating with clothing, and can project and interpret messages that are amazingly subtle and complex. But great numbers of people don't take advantage of clothing language, simply because they don't know how—or don't even realize that it exists. They just wonder why others respond to them in a less than positive way.

When a woman does not dress up to her potential, it's not necessarily due to a lack of taste, but often to a misguided sense of who she is and what she wants to tell the world. A woman's ability to reflect her inner self through clothing is also limited by ingrained attitudes that we females bring to our evaluations of our femininity and our characters. Without the rigid rules of fashion that guided our mothers and grandmothers, it's often difficult to find a personal style.

The average American woman, depending on her economic bracket, has an investment in her closet that represents anywhere from one to three thousand dollars—and she replenishes this wardrobe constantly. Yet, more likely than not, she feels she has "nothing to wear." This does not represent any of the "illogical vagaries" of the feminine temperament. Nor does it represent a greedy, acquisitive urge. In fact, it's probably quite accurate. There probably *is* something wrong with many of the garments in her closet. That dress isn't her anymore; other clothing is out-of-date, worn looking or, more likely, was a mistake in the first place.

You Probably Do *Have Nothing to Wear*

Typically, a woman's efforts to supplement her wardrobe are constrained by budget considerations and by guilt. She may hesitate to do anything because she simply doesn't know where to begin. Frequently, when she does make a purchase, she does it so haphazardly that she's only added one more mistake to her wardrobe and is more discouraged than ever.

Apart from outmoded "modeling" schools, there are really no facilities for learning style. Yet, people do want to learn. When I'm talking to a woman for the first time, no matter how well-dressed and poised she is, what I do for a living always seems to intrigue her. At most gatherings, I find myself being questioned as eagerly as a pediatrician at a suburban cocktail party.

The Stylish Don't Teach Style

I am an image consultant. I help women whose time is limited, or who feel unsure of their judgment or taste, to develop a personal style of dress that is uniquely theirs. My clients come from many professions, and for all sorts of reasons. An ambassador's wife who lectures all over the country comes for a public-speaking image, a wardrobe that will look good from afar. A young woman recently graduated from law school realizes she has never worn anything but blue jeans, and she's beginning a career in which she wants to appear sophisticated and successful. A newscaster needs nightly variety in her clothing—if only from the waist up. A dancer runs her own ballet school, and wants to be sure her look is dramatic and creative so that she can be a walking advertisement for her school. A business executive comes to me because she wants to impress her fashionable female boss with her own chic.

How Image Consulting Works

(And I must keep it confidential that her employer coincidentally is also using my services.) Many women come to me in mid-life. After many years of caring for a family, they now realize it's their turn—it's time to pay attention to themselves. Common to all my clients is a desire to take better control of their lives, to grow and to learn.

Most women come to me on their own. But occasionally a man will engage my services for his wife or daughter. More and more these days, a corporate employer invites me to advise a female executive whose clothing image is restricting her advancement in the firm. Corporations, business schools and colleges ask me to lecture to employees and students on the power of clothing language.

When I'm engaged by a new client, if it's at all possible I make a trip to her home, not just to check out her closet but also to see whether her clothing is in harmony with her environment and other expressions of herself. I ask her to try on all her clothing to see just what can be salvaged and updated, and what is just not doing anything for her image. Then the next day, alone, I research stores and boutiques all over the city, reserving a huge selection of clothes for her to choose from, always keeping in mind her personality, life-style and budget. Finally, she and I go on a whirlwind shopping spree, which can last anywhere from three hours to all day. At that point, we coordinate her entire wardrobe, so that she needn't go into a store again for the rest of that season.

At first, the client is almost always full of explanations and justifications. "I could do it perfectly well for myself if I had the time. . . ." Later, when we become friends, she confesses she really could have found the time; she just didn't know how to go about acquiring a consistent and individual image. I try to let the new client know that my aim is not to criticize, but to help. Often, all the way to the closet, she chatters nervously, apologizing for herself as if I were a house-mother coming around on an inspection tour. For some reason, women think that people in fashion are uppity and aloof. But sooner or later there is that first beautiful, genuine smile, and I know that I've broken through the barrier of mistrust, and that we've become a team. When she realizes that it's not my ego trip but hers, she relaxes. The gratification I feel when, right before me in the dressing-room mirror, a woman improves her looks—and her feelings about herself—is what keeps me going. I like clothes, but I love people, and helping them to feel better about themselves is what it's all about.

When I began my "New Image" business eight years ago, I thought it would grow by word of mouth—that clients would tell other women about my service. But I found that most women tend to keep their use of an image consultant a deep, dark secret, even from their closest friends. Somewhere along the way, we women have acquired the idea that we should have an instinctive sense of style, that it ought to be born in us as an integral part of our femininity, and that, if it is lacking, we are somehow un-womanly. I imagine that when people first began using interior decorators they felt the same vague sense of shame and inadequacy. Help with personal style is sometimes needed even more—it's far easier to be objective about a room than it is about one's own body!

As "New Image" has grown in size and scope, appearances on local and national television shows have enabled me to speak to women all over the country about personal style. After every broadcast, hundreds of women phone in with questions, and I can be sure that bundles of letters will soon arrive at my New York office. Many women cannot afford to hire a style consultant, but that doesn't mean they don't need and want help. Many make mistakes about their priorities and compromises in their images that are both detrimental and unnecessary. This book, then, is in part a response to all the inquiries which I haven't been able to answer personally; it's designed to give instruction in the clothing language in much the same way that I give it to my individual clients. It is my hope that *Looking Terrific* will shed just a little light on why women are so troubled about their body image, that it will demonstrate we're all having the same struggles and that it will convince you clothing is not a bother and a bore but a terrific way to enjoy yourself and improve the quality of your life.

In the first section of the book, you'll learn how *the language* of clothing works, how it affects your life and society and how it often controls your behavior. You'll gain valuable clues for reading the "messages" sent by others. We will examine the fascinating phenome-

How to Read This Book

non of fashion, both past and present, so that you can adapt it to your needs, rather than being ruled by it.

Part Two of our book concerns *you*. We'll talk about all the factors in a woman's life which contribute to her body and clothing image, and why it's more difficult for a woman to express a clear clothing message than for a man. You'll have an opportunity to learn more about the inner you—to set some goals and to decide which aspects of yourself you'd like to project in your clothing image.

Section Three of *Looking Terrific* puts *you* and the *language* together. Here we get down to specifics of body proportion, how to disguise faults and enhance assets. You'll learn a plan for a basic wardrobe that will work for you anywhere. Together we'll go through your closet to weed out items which no longer say "you," and we'll organize and update items that do. Then, taking into account the special needs and priorities of your life-style, I'll help you plan exciting and practical additions to your new wardrobe. As one who makes her living at shopping, I'll let you in on some secrets that can demystify that often traumatic process. Finally, we'll integrate that new clothing into your wardrobe and your daily routine, and set you on your way toward an enriched future in which you and your clothing image will continue to evolve.

To gain the most benefit from the book, it's important that you learn each lesson in order. So don't cheat and go right to the specific tips on dressing. This is not a beauty book, or just a set of how-to instructions, but a whole process of change, from the inside out. Creating and maintaining a personal style takes time and commitment, but you suspected that even before you picked this book up; one must always make an investment to get a return. A style may look effortless— that's just the way it's supposed to look—but it's not. What it takes is the will to try.

No woman should feel guilty about spending time on herself. Style is not a frivolous or foolish occupation. It's as basic as our human need for self-fulfillment. As our globe becomes more and more crowded, as cultures become frighteningly homogeneous, our individuality becomes more precious to us, and dress is one very vital way of expressing that individuality.

To begin, just for fun and maybe a little self-enlightenment, try answering a few questions which may tell you something about the present state of your clothing image and your skills in the art of dressing.

1. Do you often apologize for, or feel you have to justify, the way that you're dressed?

2. Do you attract people with whom you have interests in common? Or are you constantly having to fend off those who are not your type? On a date, do men often misunderstand the agenda for the evening?

3. When you catch an unexpected glimpse of yourself in a mirror, do you like what you see? Are you threatened by women who are dressed well? How often, really, do you walk down the street feeling totally together?

4. Is the daily act of dressing a pleasure, or do you tend to get frantic when you're getting ready to go out?

5. Can you be ready in half an hour for almost any occasion, or are you refusing to go places because you "don't have the right thing to wear"?

6. Do you decide every day what impression you want to create? Or do you just put on what's there?

7. Are you getting value for what you're spending on clothes? How many mistakes are hanging in your closet right now?

8. Can you be manipulated by relatives or sales clerks into buying and wearing garments you don't like? Do you get headaches in department stores?

9. Are you attracting the attention that you want and need and deserve in your life, or are you the one that people just naturally ignore? Do waiters take their time getting to your table? Do people shove ahead of you in the supermarket line?

10. Do you have a sneaking suspicion that the way you look is dull, that you're boring the world?

If your responses indicate that clothing may be more of a problem than a pleasure for you, *Looking Terrific* can help.

So whether you're a fashion nut or a barefoot, blue-jeans baby; whether you want to take on the dressing game to express yourself artfully, to help your career, to elicit just the right reaction from someone special; or if you are simply curious about the language of clothing—whatever your motivations, read on! This book is for every woman who wears clothes. Let's face it, we all care.

PART I
The Language

1
The Power of Your Clothing Statement

I came down on the elevator one recent morning with a dog-walking neighbor whom I'd always considered to be quite friendly. But on this particular day she hung back in the rear of the car and didn't say a word. After she got off, I asked our elevator man if there was something wrong with Mrs. Moyer. Eddie shrugged and said, "She's a funny lady—she gets moody sometimes." I thought about it, and then probed Eddie further. "Tell me, does Mrs. Moyer become her usual chatty self only when she's all dressed up?" Eddie turned around abruptly and almost shouted, "You've got it!"

Mrs. Moyer didn't want to be seen that morning because her hair was in curlers and she was sloppily dressed in a T-shirt and jeans. It was almost as though she thought she'd be invisible if she didn't speak.

The opinion of others is important, and we all want people to see only our best side. We spend much of our energy trying—through our exterior signs—to express our inner selves. Through our words, our actions and our physical appearance, we seek validation for the person within.

Of all the signals we send out to the world, the personality indicator that can be the strongest is clothing. Our clothing reveals how we *think* we look. The way we dress conveys a sense of our inner self as well, the subject of our thoughts made visible. So clothing is doubly important, its message doubly strong.

Clothing Is Often the Only Clue

At times, clothes are the only visible clues to our personalities—when we're silent and motionless, or when we're first seen from the side or from the rear. Even when other indicators are more apparent, clothing continues to make its statement. As the only totally portable example of our own sensitivity and taste, our clothing is judged by more people than will ever see our homes, our families or even our automobiles. And so it has become a major means for one human being to evaluate another. Even in a nudist camp, volumes are told by a hair ribbon or a brand of tennis shoes. Or you may be classified by your clogs!

But that isn't fair, you might protest. Is everyone so shallow and snobbish that to succeed we must cherish chic and forget substance? Why should anyone make a split-second judgment of another human being based on something as superficial as clothing? After all, it is only cloth draped on the outside of your body, and, since it's not you, why should it matter? Yet it does. The very first time a prehistoric human tied an animal skin firmly or provocatively or haphazardly over one shoulder, she was saying something about herself for all others to read. And thus the language of clothing began.

It's unrealistic to suppose that society is so enlightened that everyone has the patience to wait for you to open your mouth before making a judgment. When you go to a party and see a man wearing trousers that are wrinkled and too short, with bright white socks, you don't automatically say, "Gee, that must be a nice guy. I'd like to get to know him." Whether it's fair or not, a person's first judgment of other people is an emotional and an aesthetic one. Logic and persuasion and intellectual appreciation come later.

One Free Moment

When you first enter a room, an office, a bus or a business meeting, you have *one free moment,* one instant in which you receive the complete and undivided attention of those around you. In that instant, the people observing decide whether you are a threat or an attraction, whether you are of interest to them or not. In most cases, people make the vital decision about a stranger in less time than it takes to blink an eyelash. If you squander that one moment, you will have to work awfully hard for the next one.

I don't think the value of that free moment can be overstated, for it is surely as important as a thousand words or dozens of later opportunities. What happens during that first "free" moment will most likely affect the remainder of the relationship—if indeed there is a relationship. How many times have you heard, "When I first met him . . ." or, "The first time I saw you I thought. . . ?" And those were comments by people who stuck around to check out their first impressions. Think of the countless others who never bothered. How often do you find yourself baffled, bewildered or even hurt because the response you elicit from others is different from the one you had hoped for?

Animals wear the same clothing every day. The color and markings on their bodies trigger specific responses in other creatures, and they are not surprised by the effect that their clothing creates. However, as the only animals who choose their own plumage, we human beings are far less expert at articulating our needs and our intentions. Too frequently, our clothing sends a message contrary to our intent, and when a roomful of people start sending out messages about themselves that are unintended or incorrect, chaos ensues. That last cocktail party you attended, for example?

Sending Out Unintended Messages

Each of us has to discover exactly how clothing can express our needs and desires, how it can communicate who we *are* and what we *want.* Throughout much of human history, this whole plumage business has been largely a matter of hit or miss because we lack a highly developed instinct to guide us. However, although we are clumsy at designing our own messages, we intuitively pick up the unintended messages of others. We know when something is frightening or repellent or exciting to us. The ability to judge another creature is, after all, an instinct essential to our survival, so we react strongly to the way others dress. Sometimes that reaction is conscious and other times subconscious, but it is always important. You may think that you "never rely on first impressions" but that is not so; our reaction to a person's clothing is instinctive and involuntary.

One Set of Feathers Isn't Enough

There's another problem, too. The messages we humans communicate to one another are so complex and so varied that one set of feathers is not enough. In fact, we need a whole closetful. For we dress to demonstrate many things—to show our social origin, our artistic bent and our sexual makeup. We dress to show our politics. We dress to protest or to emulate, to attract or to intimidate. We dress to be accepted, to find security and identity in a group. Our clothing is an attraction and a distraction, a security blanket and a fantasy. Often it both reveals and conceals at the same time.

If everyone understood the clothing language and was able to use it to advantage, life would be simple, for all of us would understand at a glance where everyone else stood and where they were headed. However, far from being expert at the nuance of clothing language—though we react instinctively—most of us speak a halting pidgin clothing at best. Frustrated by our inability to communicate our selves, we even resort to message T-shirts, simply spelling out our messages across our chests for all to read. Slogans such as "My Body Belongs To Me," "Grouch" or "Unemployed Artist" may be a little crude, but they are effective, and speak out loud and clear.

You Can't Dress in a "Neutral" Way

Trying to avoid the whole issue, people often think they can stay out of trouble by dressing in a nice neutral sort of way. Unfortunately, it is not possible to dress in a neutral way; whatever you wear makes a statement of some kind. Every time you dress, you're making choices, and even an "I-don't-care" message is a clear statement.

In nature, careful grooming is basic to survival. An animal that displays a shabby coat is immediately marked as easy prey. In the same manner, when we encounter another person who is poorly dressed, we tend to discount his worth. When we see he is not up to par, we may treat him badly and degrade him even further. If you have ever been depressed and let your appearance show it, you may have experienced this phenomenon yourself.

If You've Ever Been Depressed

After one young woman's husband left her, she sank into a morass of self-pity, and almost everything she attempted turned to disaster. She sat around waiting for help, but nobody came to rescue her. She couldn't get a job, she had no money, she let her appearance go, she gained weight. We are all at least somewhat familiar with these patterns of despair. For Margaret, the depression began to lift when she exerted herself to improve her appearance. Working from the outside in, she made herself look interesting to others. That buoyed her spirits and gave her a start on the road to emotional health. Following the classic pattern of emergence from a depressed state, Margaret was saying through her improved appearance that she was ready to move on to a new place, and to leave the past behind.

Whatever aspect of yourself you display most often is also the aspect which will become stronger and stronger in your life; the role you play is the person you tend to become. Whatever you project through your clothing is, in some way, true. It is you, but is it the you that you want to project? *We can choose the qualities we feature, and it is not a lie to stress the best.* We all have both good and bad characteristics. The idea is to get some teamwork going among the various indicators of your personality, and to let clothing—the easiest of all to change—lead the way. Stress your strong points, armor your weak points, and when you are feeling down you will be protected by your clothing image and will function better.

The Role You Play Is the Person You Become

Your clothing affects your own mood at least as much as it does that of the observer. You have undoubtedly noticed the way some people tend to swagger in boots or click along efficiently in high heels. Perhaps you have also noticed that when you wear casual clothes even your spoken language tends to become more casual. Suppose you decide to stay home on a rainy Saturday and catch up on your letter-writing. If you choose to wear a crisp, clean shirt and a pair of pants, your letter will reflect a different mood than if you just bundle up in that warm, old woolly robe. The people who get your letter may never see what you are wearing, but they will certainly be affected by it.

Be aware when you change your clothing just how it affects you. When you take off an apron, does it change your mood? What does a sexy nightgown do for you? Think about the evocative power of certain fabrics and colors, sometimes evocative only to you personally, and sometimes almost universally predictable.

How Clothing Affects Your Mood

23

Probably the easiest way to invite ridicule is to behave in a way that contradicts your clothing. Be aware that when you dress each day, you are setting the parameters of your behavior. Going to the office in a cocktail dress is not only impractical, it is confusing to others.

The other day I saw a young woman on a bus, wearing a beautifully tailored suit. She was sitting with her knees together and her feet apart, heels turned over. It could have been attractive in a charming, gawky kind of way if she had been wearing a pair of corduroy overalls, but, with her sophisticated suit, it looked bizarre. People were staring, wondering what was wrong; her attitude was incongruous with her clothing.

The kind of clothing that we wear influences our habitual posture and movement. It animates or slows down the wearer. It changes the way we walk, run, bend, squat, kneel or sit. Thus, clothing has been used since time immemorial to help enforce society's rules. The dress codes we observe in restaurants, schools and private clubs are intended to control our behavior at least as much as they control our appearance.

Just as one item of clothing is dependent on the rest of the costume for its effect, so is your clothing dependent on other indicators of your personality. The messages that we convey with our clothing should harmonize with the other aspects of our personality and with the general setting. If conflicting messages are being sent—a mature person in childlike dress, frivolous clothing for serious activity, someone dressed coyly but acting aggressively—then other people are going to sense the confusion, and they may tune out, either because of mistrust or because they don't want to take the trouble to clarify the ambiguities. People read your clothing message according to the alphabet they know. So, if you build up certain expectations with your clothing, but then your actions run contrary to your clothes—or if your identity turns out to be different from what was "advertised"—people tend to become disconcerted or possibly even angry with you for disrupting their system. If you look like one of the employees, and you're actually the boss, you may incur the hostility of those who mistake your identity.

Contrary to what we may imagine, people observing us are not generally looking to see if we are a half-inch thicker in the waist than perhaps we should be. They're really not looking to see if we're wearing last season's style. What they are looking for is a harmonious whole. Whether they know it or not, they are looking to see if everything about another person points in the same direction. If the parts add up to a whole that is pleasant and exciting and interesting, then that person will be welcome company.

I like to think of our personality indicators in terms of a simple mathematical equation, in which one plus one can add up to any of several different sums. If, for example, you say one thing with your clothing image and another with other factors of your personality, you may be a walking contradiction; one plus one may add up to zero. Or if you say one thing with your personality and then make a clothing statement that agrees with it, one plus one may add up to two. However, *if what you say with your clothing enhances your personality to the maximum,* the one and one that you began with can quite magically add up to three. That is called synergy and that, as far as I'm concerned, is the name of the game. It's making the whole equal to more than the sum of its parts.

The Synergy Equation

$$1 \,\&\, 1 \approx 0$$

If you say one thing with your clothing image and another with other factors in your personality, you may be a walking contradiction.

$$1 \,\&\, 1 \approx 2$$

If you say one thing with your personality and then make a clothing statement that agrees with it, you are doing all right, but you could do better.

$$1 \,\&\, 1 \approx 3$$

If what you say with your clothing enhances your personality to the maximum, you have mastered the language of clothing.

Let's consider two women about to attend an important social event. Kate is hoping to meet a man. Wanting to be noticed and desired and courted, she wears the sexiest, clingiest outfit that she has in her closet. However, when she gets to the party, she discovers that with all that décolletage she has exposed more of herself than she wants to and now feels compelled to hide what she's got left. Because she feels vulnerable and ill at ease, she will retreat from contact with others and may appear to be arrogant and distant. Kate may meet the man of her dreams at that party, but he probably won't be interested.

Lisa, about to attend a dinner at the home of her corporation's executive vice president, has decided to play it safe in an innocuous evening skirt and plain blouse. As she enters the opulent living room and the guests raise their eyes to give her that one "free moment," she finds herself briefly inspected—and then ignored. In less than an instant, the guests are deep into their conversation again, her appearance arouses no curiosity and sustains no interest. Although that instant is almost subliminal, it proves to have an important effect on the young woman's behavior. Feeling the pain of rejection, she spends the remainder of the evening trying to regain lost ground, and finds herself moving awkwardly and talking too loudly. To her own horror, she hears herself dropping her credentials into the conversation. "When I was at Smith . . ."

When the impression we're making in the present is not working, we all tend to dip into the past for reinforcement. But that remedy seldom works, for it is who we are *now* that counts. Lisa became a self-conscious young woman who was trying too hard. When she dressed that evening, she believed she was saying, "I am a thoughtful, efficient, no-nonsense employee," which indeed she was. She had emphasized one aspect of herself to the exclusion of other qualities that were equally important—her wit, her intelligence, her charm. What Lisa's company executives saw that evening was a thirtyish female with plain brown hair, dressed in a basic navy blue shantung A-line skirt, and unexciting cream polyester shirt, navy-blue pumps and a pin on the shirt so small that it added nothing. (True, it was a real ruby, but who would have noticed?) There was a total lack of focus in Lisa's dress—no interesting print, no classy belt, no glitter of an unusual earring, no charm, no fun and no individuality. So, Lisa's colleagues and potential future allies thought subconsciously, why bother with her? Their first judgment was surely reinforced by her awkward conduct during the evening. In trying to dress the part of a perfect employee, Lisa failed to take into account that *one must first dress to please oneself*. When you wear something you don't like and don't feel good in, it is almost impossible to be fun and interesting.

Both Lisa and Kate tried for a particular effect. Both failed. If either one had taken the risk of demonstrating her own personality in her dress, her evening might have turned out quite differently. What both women lacked was personal style, a sense of knowing who they were and how to express that personality through clothing. One should aim to be not clothes-conscious or self-conscious, but, rather, conscious of *self* and how that self is projected through clothing. When this sense is developed, it becomes a tool that is immensely useful in all aspects of life.

One of the more important potential assets of clothing is the illusion which it allows. It permits us not only to specify who we are now but also the direction in which we are headed; we can wear a status we have not yet achieved. By pointing to our goal, clothing can help us reach it. Here's how.

*The Illusion
Clothing Allows*

We have said that when clothing changes, our mannerisms also change. Also, we trigger an entirely new set of reactions from other people, which then further affects our behavior.

*The Vicious Cycle
Versus
the Winner's Circle*

If you feel, for example, that your dress is unattractive, you'll tend to hide; when you hide, people react to this negative action. They ignore or they pursue, and sometimes they even attack.

However, if the effect of your clothing is positive, you gain confidence; you tend to move with more ease and speak more freely.

In which direction are you moving? Is yours the vicious cycle or the winner's circle? Do you fear success and reinforce your resolve to avoid it with mousy, shabby clothing? Are you setting too safe boundaries on your world and putting obstacles in your path? Or are you ready to seek new experiences, accept new responsibilities, enjoy new pleasures? If you are, clothing language can help you on your way.

The Winner's Circle versus
The Vicious Cycle

THE VICIOUS CYCLE

You made an unfortunate choice in clothing

You feel and act awkward or withdrawn

Others react negatively; they ignore, pursue or attack

Their reaction confirms your worst fears

You sink deeper into depression and isolation

THE WINNER'S CIRCLE

You change your clothing message for the better

Your self-image is somewhat improved; you show slight behavior change

People respond differently towards you

The way you feel about yourself is further enhanced; you function better; your situation improves; you identify more with success

You are ready to take the next step

2

Reading Other People's Clothing Messages

The other day, when I walked into a fashion executive's Manhattan office, I could tell immediately that she had mastered the game. Sitting proudly at a large desk placed strategically in a luxuriously decorated room, she wore a bright cerise linen suit with a huge white flower pinned to her lapel. Her surroundings and her outfit both said power. They said, "You'd better look out because I'm in charge here." In my simple little mauve dress, I would have been in real trouble had I not been able to identify the message—and then disregard it. We were two equal women, meeting to discuss a matter of interest to both of us, and so we did.

By sharpening your knowledge of the language, you can learn things about a person's basic emotional makeup, his or her mood, habits and priorities. The extent to which you refine your natural abilities and observations is up to you. I can spell out some of the rules, but it takes each person's perception to interpret—and benefit from the subtleties of the language.

To avoid being manipulated by someone else's clothing message, the first step is to raise one's own instinctive reaction from the subconscious to the conscious mind, so that it can be analyzed and dealt with in a logical way. Often we tend to overreact to some clothing messages because of stimulation from earlier memories. Learn to recognize how you react to various stimuli, and train yourself to accept or disregard the message you perceive. Or, better yet, learn to perceive the real message underlying the apparent one. The brilliant cerise of the fashion executive's costume spoke power, but the very blatancy of the message also whispered insecurity.

The Obvious Is Not Always So

In reading clothing language, the obvious is not always what it would seem. It is simple enough to assume that red means aggressive, that a high-necked gown means repressed, but this may not be the case. Red may just as well mean false bravado, and a high neck may indicate a sore throat. A covered-up gown does not necessarily mean a woman is feeling protective; if the texture is light and airy, her mood may be quite adventurous. So be sure to consider all the clues before jumping to a conclusion.

Our automatic reaction to clothing stimuli is strong. Some colors have a demonstrable physiological effect. The sight of red, for instance, changes heart and respiration rates, and may raise our blood pressure. The next time you go to a parade, be aware of the intense impact that a brightly colored uniform can have. Notice that a tall fur hat is just naturally imposing, and that brass buttons dazzle the eye. Uniforms speak an elementary language, often imbuing the wearer with a rank and authority he would not otherwise possess.

It's fairly easy to read these signs and signals. But there are numerous other ways in which people assert control and power through their clothing. Our means of asserting superiority through clothing can be almost unspoken—the quiet, impeccable designer sweater with matching skirt and just a bit of expensive jewelry. Or sometimes it is shouted—with fashionable status signatures emblazoned all over everything.

Wearing Your Occupation

Some people seek to achieve recognition by wearing their occupations on their sleeves, which is fine unless it becomes a caricature. Too much the tweedy journalist, the Wall Street stockbroker or the energetic jock, and one suspects a basic weakness in self-identity. Take away the occupation and what have you got? I'm put in mind of a lawyer who wears her attractive, silky harem pajamas to a party, but then tops them with her professional blazer—just in case anybody should doubt her authenticity. This is very much like the woman who continues to wear her fur stole indoors as a mark of her station.

Hats also have a way of conferring instant identity or authority. Some people have built an entire reputation around a hat. Hat people are customarily individualists, and the hat can be quite an effective way of demonstrating one's style—and one's humor. But watch out when a hat becomes pure costume. The man who affects a 1930's panama may really wish he were a movie star, and he may be so busy with that fantasy he has trouble dealing with the here and now. Dark glasses are another variation on the theme, an easy way of conferring rank or creating drama for the wearer. They are also an excellent way of keeping others discomfited, or guessing at your mood or motive.

Some people get pleasure and power from the negative attention clothing can attract. The man who wears an oversized plaid in bright green, the teenager in a psychedelic T-shirt—these people are probably not concerned with your approval: their intent is simply to invade your space, force your attention and thus manipulate your behavior. In this they almost always win.

Getting Negative Attention

The person who constantly affects different roles through clothing may simply be demonstrating different aspects of himself or herself, which would indicate a basic sureness about his or her identity. But constantly changing images may also indicate a search for identity. Important clues can be gained not just from the clothing itself but from the context in which it is worn. Is a person in harmony or at odds with his or her "silent partner"? Is he or she too conscious of clothing? Does she preen? Does she sit or stand to show the clothing to advantage, or does she attempt to conceal it? Is that stranger you're watching having a quarrel with his ill-fitting, uncomfortable shoes? Did he choose to make himself uncomfortable, and why? Sometimes people in need of physical reinforcement caress or stroke their clothing. Others abuse it, and this also says something about their character. Has a person chosen a garment that will allow her to be relaxed about what she is doing? Is her clothing in tune with the tastes she's expressed in

Different Roles Through Clothing

her life-style, her living room? If not, there may be a conflict somewhere.

Where's Your "Equity"? Another very useful way to read personality through clothing is to determine in what aspect of self the person has placed his or her "equity." What is it that he wants the world to see? Most people, either consciously or unconsciously, habitually choose clothing that points up one facet of their physical self or their psyche. A woman may be extremely proud of a full bosom, or beautiful legs, or she may want to display sensitivity and artistry through unusual fabrics and designs.

Naomi has dark and exotic features and she chooses clothing that sets off her face well. Her apparel is never cluttered or busy at the neck, nor is it clothing worn simply for its own sake. Rather, it always provides a "clean canvas," a dramatic setting for a striking face. Her hair pulled back to the nape of her neck, her makeup, her earrings, her necklace—all these join to lead you to her face. Years ago, because of her outstanding features, Naomi made the choice to place her equity in her face.

Gwen, equally attractive, wears her straight hair loose and flowing free; her face is nearly devoid of makeup, and she chooses clothing that conforms closely to her figure. She'll favor slacks for everyday wear and for special occasions body-hugging evening gowns. Gwen is athletic and moves well. The statement she makes to the world is, "I'm healthy, and I rejoice in my beautiful body."

If you were to analyze the faces and bodies of both these women, you'd realize that, although Naomi's face is indeed lovely, her body is equally as attractive. You're just never quite as aware of that because of the equity point she has chosen. Gwen's face would be far more exciting, too, had she chosen to accent it with makeup and hairdo. Early choices about our "equity" point can have a profound effect upon the way our personalities (and our lives) develop.

The decision we make about where we place our equity very often survives after the logical reason for it has disappeared. We've all seen the woman still proudly displaying a figure that no longer warrants display, or an ingenue charm that has long since faded. There are important reasons why our clothing image—and our self-image—must constantly evolve and grow.

Clothing not only shows what portion of the body or the psyche a person wishes to emphasize, but it can also help to determine where in her appearance a woman's anti-equity point is—of what feature she is most ashamed. The extreme is a woman wishing to hide her whole body. She may wear dark clothing with a focal point near the face, or she may emphasize her hands through gestures, jewelry and nail polish. Sometimes people also attempt to hide natural qualities of their personality. With incongruously bland clothing they attempt to disguise temper, or they hide irresponsibility with sober, "respectable" garb. People who fear competition may wear clothing for camouflage, choosing heavy materials, murky colors and loose shapes.

Color is an important element in the language of clothing. In fact, some would call it a complex language all its own. Red is an "advancing" color and gives the sensation of warmth. It has traditionally represented courage, and suggests an extroverted and optimistic mood. Yellow seems nearly always to have been identified with the mind and the intellect. Purple has been thought of as a color of high rank, and blue is associated with the spiritual and celestial. But, along with these general assumptions, there are some inconsistencies. Since ancient times, the "spiritual" color, blue, has also been traditionally assigned to workmen (the "blue-collar" worker). Green is supposed to bring tranquility and calm, but, as you know, only some greens are peaceful; others can be almost blinding in their intensity, so the shade of the color is vital to its interpretation. I believe that colors and the shades one chooses say more about one's mood than about one's personality.

Color: A Language All Its Own

Individuals vary in their perception of color, and the meaning that they attach to a particular hue is often dependent on past associations and experiences, or influenced by the fabric or design of a garment or by current fashion. (When a particular shade is "in," all rules are "out.") The color language, then, is very much like music—the same note may be played in different ways, with different meanings for different people. Again, be aware of the context.

Often, your skill at interpreting the clothing language may make a large difference in your ability to relate to others. Take the situation of

Understanding Others' Messages

a first day on a new job. You can size up the people you'll be working with from the way they have chosen to frame their egos. As you walk into the office, the first person you encounter is the receptionist. She can be important to you, either as an ally or as a foe. This one is the heavily armored type, a super-corseted lady with permanent indentations on her shoulders from straps straining to hold the whole thing together. Perhaps she has denied herself the physical part of life altogether; forty years may pass without the sun or wind touching her skin. Those tight-fitting straps and lacings represent a cautious and continuous, albeit impersonal, embrace. More than likely, if you make an extra effort to be thoughtful to this woman, she'll be your friend.

Consistency of Taste   As an example of how consistent people's clothing choices are with other preferences, you'll notice that people who wear protective clothing frequently prefer small, protective, dim-lit rooms. If they are very covered up by clothes, they are probably also protective of their thoughts and feelings. On the other hand, people who wear open and exposed clothing tend to enjoy wide, airy spaces. Take a poll; you'll see!

Soft textures in attire tend to invite human contact and closeness. Crisp textures show that a person wants to be regarded as efficient (and from a certain distance). Also, the lines of clothing, whether they are strict or flowing, provide some indication of how rigid the personality is.

The office manager, a woman in her forties, is wearing basic black and one large piece of jewelry. This indicates that she is pretty sure of herself—it's a limited look but she's got it down. Her whole wardrobe is basically dark, to show off the ethnic treasures she's collected in her world travels. She is an effective and strong personality, and you can probably count on her to be straightforward in manner. Another woman wearing a lot of clanking jewelry seems to be actively seeking attention. Don't step on her turf!

You are going to hire an assistant and you interview three people for the job. The first has obviously invested a good deal of effort in putting together a look, but somehow, instead of being integrated and harmonious, it simply looks contrived. This woman's script says "try, try, and almost succeed." She is the type who will put in an eighty-hour work week for you mostly in wasted motion, and get very little done.

I would also not select the woman in the severely cut maroon gabardine suit which makes her look for all the world like a Swiss railway conductor. She is trying so hard to appear professional that no one is going to be able to respond to her as a person; this is not someone you want to work with day after day.

A third interviewee has taken the trouble to find out what the people in this company customarily wear, and she will combine that knowledge with her own style and taste. If it is a suit, then she is confidently attired in that. If it is more casual then she may be wearing a good-looking wool skirt and a matching soft silk blouse. Neither her clothing nor hairstyle require any adjusting during the interview. (Nervous mannerisms, such as pushing hair out of the eyes or rearranging one's dress, have discouraged many an otherwise eager employer.) If this applicant's qualifications measure up to her clothing sense, then she may be a good bet for the job.

In your work at this office, your knowledge of clothing language will be useful not only in gaining some initial understanding of people, but also in dealing on a daily basis with them. Even small changes in the way an associate looks from day to day can signal other changes that may be important to you. A luncheon partner who has deliberately chosen a completely uncharacteristic type of dress for the occasion is probably demonstrating vulnerability; the meeting may be more vital to him or her than it is to you.

Reading Your Co-workers' Moods

Next time you're on a bus or sitting in your doctor's office, why not make use of the empty moments to sharpen your powers of observation and come up with some interesting revelations about human nature?

As you learn to interpret ever more subtle messages from others, remember that you are transmitting equally revealing messages yourself. Through a fuller understanding of the uses of fashion and the language of clothing, you can learn to tailor these messages to elicit just the responses you want.

3

The Fashion Game

Do you ever go into a store and feel yourself bombarded from all sides with the same "in" fashion look? It seems impossible to buy anything in a different style. When the current fashion look is simply not for us, we begin to wonder just what the point of fashion is, anyhow. Besides increasing our gross national product, besides enriching manufacturers, besides causing a lot of waste and headaches and planned obsolescence, what does fashion really do for us? Why can't each of us simply adopt a personal style that's creative and expressive of our personality, and let it go at that? Why? Because fashion is stimulating and useful. Because the changes that are fundamental to fashion are also essential and integral to society. Once you understand the phenomenon of fashion, you should no longer feel intimidated or insecure. Inspired by fashion, you will be able to blend your own taste and style with the knowledge of what can and should, according to the temper of the times, be worn in a given setting. That's more than fluency in the clothing language—that's eloquence.

Anatole France, the great turn-of-the-century novelist, said that if he were transported to another age, he would first pick up a women's fashion magazine, for that would tell him more about humanity's changes than any of the philosophers, novelists, prophets or scholars. Clothing *is* important. When you think about another period of history—colonial days, for example—isn't your first image that of the *clothing* that was worn then?

Fashion is more than a barometer of the times; it not only reflects history, it sometimes can contribute to making it happen. Many a dissident group first took hold when it discovered that one of the most effective ways to give their movement identity and strength was through distinctive dress. Look at the sixties' hippie movement—a revolution that began with blue jeans and went on to change national events.

Fashion Contributes to History

Fashion has existed for nearly as long as clothing; early man apparently put on clothing as much out of the desire to create a fashion as for warmth or to cover his "shameful" nakedness. There seem to be as many theories about why we wear clothing as there are anthropologists to propound them. So if you were to assume that we adopted clothing only to cover our bodies, or to keep warm, you would be wrong. In fact, some authorities have suggested, in all seriousness, that clothing came into use originally because of man's need for pockets!

Surely the desire to beautify was also important. The word, garb, means graceful outlines, and raiment means to array oneself. Throughout history, the functional considerations of clothing have nearly always taken a back seat to the aesthetic. As the normally staid *Encyclopaedia Britannica* remarks in a rare burst of poetic enthusiasm, "clothing is not merely a covering of the body, but a vesture of the soul."

Since primitive times, important events have always been occasions for special attention to the body. The behavior of people when they're "dressed up" differs from their normal conduct, and their state of mind is conditioned by the awareness of their special appearance.

Sometimes people dress as a pure expression of their desire to create something of beauty. Generally, however, our urge to dress attractively is outwardly directed. Most clothing is designed for its use in social interaction and, when best used, enhances and advances the individual.

Men's clothing predominantly expresses pride or class. Among primitive groups, rank was indicated by the number and size of feathers

Status: The Primary Clothing Message

or ornaments a man wore. Wearing a "feather in his cap" made a man look taller and more decorative. It also tended to make other men jealous—and a man had to fight for his right to wear them. Thus, the number of feathers worn came to indicate the wearer's strength and success. These days, military rank is displayed with gold braid, badges and ribbons, and civilian rank through more subtle, but equally unmistakable means. Status is still the primary male message.

Clothing of high rank for both males and females has always been deliberately designed to be fragile and easily dirtied, and to restrict physical activity, perhaps to prove that the wearer doesn't have to work. Usually it has been unwise, or even downright risky, to assume the dress of another class or station, either up or down the scale. How many stories can you think of based on this prince-and-pauper theme, in which members of the upper or lower class get themselves into trouble by masquerading as one another?

Since men's clothing is based on class forms, and since class forms resist change, men's fashions have tended to alter more slowly than women's. In countries with little social upheaval, fashions remained unchanged for hundreds of years.

Another original motive for wearing clothing was as protection against the supernatural. It was one of early man's means of defending himself against evil spirits and appeasing his gods. Today we still wear copper bracelets for health, elephant hair for good luck and religious medals. And how many of us have a "lucky" garment, a sweater or a golf cap, which "protects" us in tricky situations?

Some scientists, discounting magic, aesthetics, pockets and class as the raison d'être of clothing, believe that, in the final analysis, dress is a means of expressing sexual energy. Women's clothing especially, they point out, has followed the principle of seduction.

Shifting Erogenous Zones in Female Clothing

A psychologist of dress, John Flügel, explains the changes in female fashions by his theory of "shifting erogenous zones." To the modern mind, the *removal of clothing* is of erotic significance, but in truth, he says, it is *covering a part* of the body which makes it exciting. Dr. Flügel believes that every part of the female body is essentially erotic to the male. Through fashion we direct attention to different parts of our body at different times. When we hide a portion of our anatomy it becomes mysterious and desired. Then later, by uncovering it, or by outlining it in tight clothing, that built-up erotic tension is exploited. We all know how exciting it is on the first warm day of spring when women take off their coats. In April, even the hint of a thigh is provocative, but by August the sight of a woman's legs in even the shortest shorts evokes only yawns.

The shifting erogenous zones Dr. Flügel describes have no particular logic about them; they tend to migrate all over the body. If caught without her veil an Arab woman will lift her skirt and expose her body to cover her face. Even as late as the early 1900's, the European woman who proudly displayed great mounds of quivering bosom would blush if she thought someone had caught sight of her ankle.

The numerous and varied reasons for wearing clothing will continue to exist for as long as society exists but the order of their priority changes constantly. That's one of the things that makes life interesting. Just now, with the ease of travel, with social mobility, with generally higher living standards for all, dress has become less important as an indicator of social class. Mass-produced clothes are available worldwide; Paris originals are ripped off overnight and sold at 'bargain' prices. Thus, communications and modern manufacturing are both great leveling influences.

What's more, as our sexual attitudes shift, men's clothing is becoming more colorful and more alluring, and the ensnaring aspect of women's fashions is loosening up, giving way to a more honest expression of sexuality. And so, as rigid class structure and traditional sexual roles change, clothing becomes more an expression of the person and consequently an even more effective tool for self-fulfillment.

It used to be that fashion was more influenced by place than by time; fashions of a particular locale, which remained unchanged for decades, differed from those of another village nearby. Fashion was the way you knew who the out-of-towners were. While that is still true to some extent, fashion is far more universal today. Change in fashion is influenced by war, by economic conditions, by technological advances. During the first World War, when that independent lady, Alice Roosevelt Longworth, decided that the American woman should sacrifice her steel-boned corsets for the war effort, the grand gesture was

How and Why Fashion Changes

enthusiastically endorsed by millions of American women. It was said to have released twenty-eight thousand tons of steel—as well as unknown quantities of flesh—to the war effort.

Early in this century, the growth of the union movement in this country made work clothes respectable, and this eventually spawned the denim revolution.

During the Depression years, curiously enough, women's clothing seemed designed to be seen from the back—which may have been our way of turning our back on the depressing times.

World War II's fabric shortages inspired a government decree that skirts would henceforth be limited to seventy-two inches around the hem. Extra ornaments, such as ruffles and cuffs, disappeared, and bare legs were seen for the first time. (Women painted seams on the backs of their made-up legs to simulate hosiery.) Daytime clothing converted to evening wear with the removal of a jacket or a bolero—remember those old Claudette Colbert and Joan Crawford films?

Technological developments during World War II were turned to civilian interests after 1945, producing that most practical of materials, wash and wear. With new types of fabric construction, better blends and new knitting and weaving techniques, easy-care wardrobes arrived and synthetics became the great leveler. Even people who could afford the authentic fabrics began to wear their imitations. Now we no longer judge a person by the authenticity of the fabric or jewelry she is wearing, but rather by how she is wearing the item. If a garment is worn with style, then the *wearer* is authentic.

The fifties brought the suburban boom: good times, lots of babies and a casual, conservative way of life. Conformity was in, and teenagers painstakingly mimicked one another with full circle skirts and saddle shoes and peter pan collars. With fads so strict they weren't even fun, the insistence on conformity inevitably led to the clothing rebellion of the sixties. The long-haired hippie, who may have begun his protest as a statement about haircuts, went on to become an activist for ideological change in the war protest and civil rights movements of the sixties.

Just about anything around us can affect fashion. The sudden prominence of a person, place or event, the popularity of a play, a resort, a film, an exhibit or a song, can give rise to a new fashion. The price of oil raises our heating bills, and we see fleecy, warm fabrics in the new designs. Layered clothing becomes the style. Recession and a growing fear of violence on the streets makes it necessary for chic to become discreet. Even though it doesn't always seem so, there's a rhyme and reason behind it all.

As the pace of life speeds up, fashion's pace is becoming faster than ever before. Because of tremendous media exposure, as well as contact with others' life-styles, we're becoming more and more fickle in our tastes and will change our clothing on a moment's notice—just as soon as some kind of sanction for that change has been granted. We see something on television, and rush out the next day to buy it—anything to be ahead in the fashion game. This is fine, so long as we don't follow blindly, so long as our choice is in harmony with our own aesthetic tastes and the image we want to project. These are fast-moving and competitive times, but they can also be looked on as exciting, and potentially creative.

The Ever-Quickening Pace

To understand the mechanics of fashion change, and avoid some of the pitfalls, let's trace the genesis of a new fashion—from the time it's just a gleam in a couturier's eye until it takes over your local department store.

The Birth of a New Look

In preparing their new collections, designers attempt to maintain the utmost secrecy, but somehow or other what one couturier produces in a given season often seems to bear a striking resemblance to that of all the other designers. That's due in part to the fact that all of them are influenced by the same world conditions. They read the same press, watch the same television, see the same fabric collections and are undoubtedly influenced by other designers' successful collections of the previous year; everyone wants to be a winner.

With the major Paris designers now heavily involved in mass merchandising, haute couture design has become more of a giant PR effort than a profitable business in itself. Profits these days are derived from the spurred sales of these same designers' less expensive ready-to-wear collections, accessories, sheets, towels and what-have-you. This expansion, incidentally, began in the 1960s when the social revolution forced the couture houses to get into "affordable" ready-to-wear. French

41

fashion houses will earn more than a billion dollars this year on their mass production items; they'll lose heavily on their couture collection. Increasingly, their "creations" are designed to make news, rather than to be practical and wearable. To get the free "advertising" of media attention, designers vie with one another for a way-out look or a gimmicky idea.

The fashion industry is so competitive that each designer's show must be bigger and more of an extravaganza than the last. Attention focuses on who is showing where, how many models and which ones. One model recently told me that, at her fashion house, basic design now takes second place to creative accessorizing for a show to make the garment sell. Just "get some fabric on her body and then we'll start with the fun stuff"—deciding what shoes, scarves and belt to add. And so, for the first time since tailoring replaced draping of clothes as early as the thirteenth century, much of the look of a garment is left to the wearer. But, leave it to fashion—next year all this may change.

The designer's model, who is often relied upon for inspiration and sometimes consulted about a design, is supposed to present "an interesting image," and yet allow the clothes to be the important thing. A few models have become more important than the clothes. They are the superstars of the fashion world, and it is their prominence which has upset the old status quo.

In the past, the model who sold the most clothes was the most successful. Now it's the model who gets the most press coverage, the girl with the most spectacular style, the girl who's the best dancer or gyrator. Whatever it is she does, she does in a flamboyant way, and that gets the name of the designer before the public. To make the clothes come alive, the model now often has to be wild in her movements, particularly if the design has little or no construction.

The press, of course, is delighted with this approach. Editors are always looking for stories, and with the power they hold to provide space for fashion news, or withhold it, they wield a tremendous influence on our fashions. Their tendency is to promote the more bizarre styles—the ones that make the most interesting copy.

Designs that have been given the best press coverage at the Paris openings are then picked up by the Seventh Avenue manufacturers, who produce their own slightly modified versions. Department store buyers are given a preview of these designs, but only the styles they select in large enough quantities are made up. Sometimes as much as a third of a line is eliminated because there are too few orders to warrant production. Thus majority taste rules (at least the store's view of what majority taste may be) and the consumer's selection is limited. Even the purchaser's choice in size is often restricted; designers do not like their clothing seen on, or photographed on, heavy women; if designers had their way, all of us would transform ourselves into a tall size eight. Even when a full range of sizes is manufactured, too often all of them are constructed to suit the proportions of the tall, willowy woman. Other types would at least have a chance to look attractive in that fashion if it were cut to their proportions.

Some female designers tend to be a bit more practical than men in their clothing design. After all, for them it's not fantasy; many of the females first became involved in designing in order to solve their own body problems, and you'll notice their line of clothing generally flatters their own body type.

There will always be new noise and excitement in fashions, for that's the way the industry charges itself up—and gives us a lift, too. Choices for the consumer at any one time, however, tend to be limited to variations on a theme.

The media, through advertising, constantly urge purchase of the latest fashions, subtly discouraging us from any independence. The media is a powerful influence, indeed, with television alone capturing our attention for a staggering forty-nine hours a week of average family viewing. This enormous impact upon our sensibilities has produced a nation of women insecure about their image, and willing to spend a disproportionate share of their time, their income and their energy often just mindlessly buying whatever is current—and feeling pushed around in the process. They don't realize it's not necessary to be a slavish devotee of fashion. Women *can* refuse to wear fashions which are uncomfortable, which limit physical activity, which are stifling or lack dignity—you just refuse to buy. Fashions may be set by the designer, but they are bought only by us, the consumer. Or not bought. For example, in the summer of 1970, French designers, unhappy with miniskirts, let hemlines fall, and American designers felt

A Rose
Between the Teeth
and Other Excesses

compelled to follow. But the designers were following their whims instead of their instincts, and womanhood rebelled en masse. Rejecting the long skirts, we took to pants, thus making a strong statement of independence.

While fashions depicted by the media may capture your imagination, how do you reinterpret the image of that lovely lady in *Vogue,* for example, who is standing in a gale-force wind with six scarves wrapped around her throat and a flower between her teeth? Being a stand-in for a vase may look charming, but it does tend to inhibit conversation. *No one* in real life looks like high-fashion models do. But before you condemn the photographers for taking all of those outlandish and bizarre shots, do recall that it's necessary to overstate any new message for it to be understood. The real job of a fashion magazine is to stimulate and inform. You must learn to take the visual poetry of high fashion and translate it into prose to make it appropriate for you.

If you have a limitless supply of money, of course, you can follow wherever fashion leads, adopting the prefab fashion uniform of the day that's been churned out for you—and a few million other women—by the industry. But a fashion uniform is like any other; it tends to reduce the individual ego. Your "very latest" may attract attention—but to you or to itself? If you invest your equity in slavishly following the fashion of the moment, it is the *costume* which will carry the authority. *You* will become the mannikin. Far better to listen to what fashion dictates, and then respond with your own individual words and phrases.

There's an important distinction between being merely fashionable and being both chic and current; that is—*having* style and *using* fashion. Style comes from within; fashion is imposed from without. In the vast middle ground which separates the fashion uniform and anarchy, there's enormous freedom for expression of individual style.

Planned Obsolescence   How do we avoid buying clothing that will be obsolete before we get it hung up in the closet? Be aware of the fashion scene. Keep up-to-date on what's happening, but don't buy too heavily into the look which may or may not last. It's important in some circles to make the statement that you know what is current, but often a single purchase can accomplish that. If the new look is one you've awaited for years,

44

you may want to invest heavily in it because it's right for you (and then hope that it sticks around). Even if it goes out of fashion, it can often be adapted as your classic. Through it all, it is essential that you know whom you are presenting.

One bright note in the fashion scene: recently, some of the most successful designers have been those who give women a choice of many different separates, so that they can pull their own look together in a personal way. These designers know we are leaving the age of the dictated "uniform" behind. Incidentally, never buy designer labels just for the security of the name—but only if a style and special quality is right for you. Think about what you may be spending just for that little label (which I generally advise my clients to remove from the clothing anyhow, so it won't stick out accidentally, or show through sheer material). Why pay for it if you don't have to?

To stay current on the latest fashions, I would recommend reading *Vogue, Harper's Bazaar, Glamour, Mademoiselle* and, if you're pre-high school graduation, *Seventeen.* The consumer edition of the trade bible, *Women's Wear Daily,* called *WWD,* could probably keep you current all by itself. It's largely visual, very easy to read.

Keeping Up with the Times

Don't, however, confuse the *editorial pages* of a fashion magazine with the *advertising pages.* What is shown on these advertising pages is what a manufacturer has to offer. He has done his best to appraise and predict, but he is not always a fashion authority. Also, what is selected and exposed to you on the editorial pages may unfortunately be influenced by which manufacturer has taken the most advertising in the magazine.

A few more cautions. Remember that a photo does not always tell the truth about the exact shape and fit of a dress. I know from my days as a photography stylist just how many clothespins and straight pins are hidden behind a model's back. Photography in fashion magazines is frequently so arty that it's blurred, or the model is jumping two feet off the ground in hysterical glee. The public gets enchanted by a glamorous illusion, and goes to the advertised store to try to find the outfit (which may be quite a feat in itself); then the outfit doesn't fit as the consumer thought it would. In this era of mass production and poorly fitted clothes, in all too many cases it's the model and her movement that create the excitement and the illusion of glamour.

When the average woman tries the dress on, nothing happens in the mirror, but what can she expect if she just *stands* there. Some of my clients are embarrassed to move around in front of a mirror; it seems vain. But much of the new clothing looks good only in motion—(and I admit, it can become exhausting!).

To get the best of what fashion has to offer, try to remember to keep track of what looks good to your eye in stores, on television and in films, as well as on the streets. Find out what you're afraid of wearing. If you're not sure of whether you can wear a certain line, try it on in the stores. You'll soon develop your judgment to the point where, when a new line comes out, you'll know immediately whether or not it's right for you. Remember, though, with a new skirt length or a drastically new style, it takes time before your eyes have had a chance to adjust.

It's all called keeping up with the times, and it's part of what makes the world go 'round. Changing fashion? It's fascinating, and it's fun. If you blend inspiration from within with that ever-changing inspiration from without, fashion is worthwhile and exciting. It constantly gives us new aspects of the human form to view. And it's our way of adding identity to each era that passes.

PART II
You

4
Women's Changing Self-Image

When we talk about bodies and clothing, we touch every female's deepest doubt. Clothing is an extension of the body, so if you don't like your body you probably have trouble with your clothing image, too.

Women have been required for so long to fulfill the roles of sex object and ornament that they suffer far more than men do from a sense of inadequacy about their bodies. If you're an ornament, after all, it's just about impossible to be perfect enough.

Somebody once said, "Show me a woman who's not ashamed of her body and I'll show you a six-year-old child." Every woman I've ever met is insecure about at least one aspect of her body. Many of them have no faults of any particular significance (at least I can't see them), but that doesn't seem to matter. They are convinced their bodies are unattractive. And, of course, reality for one's self is what one believes.

A few years ago, when many of us were growing up, modesty was very important. Even dressing for gym class could be a real trauma; we'd clutch our towels around ourselves and scurry to cover up, losing one of the few chances we ever had to see what other female bodies looked like. The boys in the locker room next door may have been a

Such Shame
About Our Bodies

47

bit rowdy, but at least they were getting used to their own bodies, and others'.

I think it's unfortunate that women aren't more at home with the natural female form, because it has an inherent grace and integrity, a fluidity, logic and seemliness that we should appreciate. If we were comfortable with our bodies, perhaps we'd understand better how to flatter and enhance them, rather than to try to hide and disguise them.

The little girl who, at age eleven, picked up the idea that she was too thick around the middle will probably always believe it. It's almost as if women want their assumptions about their body inferiorities to be fact. We make up our faces, bedeck ourselves with jewelry, try to hide our flaws and dress as seductively as we can. But when a man tells us how beautiful we are, we don't believe him. That inconsistency follows us throughout our lives. We want to look good and to attract, yet we're embarrassed when we do. How many women have you seen who wear very short skirts, and then constantly tug at them to make them cover just a little more of their knees?

The assaults upon our body image come from all sides and at all ages. In adolescence, most of us were influenced by our mothers' attitudes toward beauty and sexuality. If the mother has difficulty in accepting less than perfection in herself, she may also resent her less-than-perfect daughter. Daddy, also, has his own inimitable way of putting daughter down. Attempting to deal with their daughters' developing womanhood, fathers often tend to make their compliments backhanded: "What did you do to your hair?" "That dress is a little tight, isn't it?" And schoolyard jokes about those "two fried eggs on your chest," or "the beard on Brenda's knees" don't seem to help a whole lot, either.

How We've Been Fantasized by Men and the Media

The standards of beauty have always been dictated by men. The criteria on which we make our decisions as to what is beautiful have been formulated from a male point of view. The icy-cold model of the sixties reflected the male's view of women: something to display and not to relate to.

36-24-36 perfection still seems expected of us all, and women are constantly put in the position of comparing themselves with their husband's favorite *Playboy* centerfold. Some women report to me that their body image remained fairly secure until pregnancy, when perhaps one thoughtless remark from the husband was enough to destroy their pride. "After I stopped nursing the baby," a client told me, "I never stopped wearing a bra, even to bed. Jack had convinced me that my breasts were ruined."

Advertising and the mass media haven't done very much to help women with their image, either. In fact, their persuasive propaganda has encouraged a vague sort of shame about even having a body. All those ads for deodorants and "personal products" can make you feel your body is an embarrassing secret, rather than a source of pride.

Back in the fifties and sixties, though fashion decreed it was okay to have breasts (those unreal, pointed ones you may remember), nipples were in poor taste. I was just out of college, working with the Bloomingdale's executive training squad in the lingerie department, when we had the first gala press showing of Rudi Gernreich's new no-bra look. I still remember the horrified gasps from the audience when the first model made her way down the runway in see-through splendor.

Also, back in those days, it was considered just "okay" to have a rear end, mostly for wearing knitted suits. But it had to be a securely encased, one-piece rear end, shaped by your latex panty girdle. No hint of a division was allowed.

As fashion changes, so different body types come in and out of vogue. But since we can't trade in our bodies for new models each year, there seems to be no way to win. We need to have big bosoms today and none tomorrow. We need to be thin with a flat chest, a wasp waistline, long legs, a swan neck. ... As we're pushed and pulled, molded and extruded into just about every shape possible, it's no wonder we feel there must be something wrong with us. The perfection demanded is never attainable. It's a continuing struggle between what we are and how we've been fantasized, both by men and by the the media, and it's done significant damage to our individual—and collective—self-esteem.

We may believe that we've arrived at a point of equality for women, and indeed we're getting there. But when this book went to print, woman was still encouraged to think that she will find social position and identity through what Simone de Beauvoir calls "her dream of unearned success." So long as we perpetuate the custom of glorifying "first ladies" and wives of important men, little girls will believe that, if they wait and get beautiful, their destinies will be fulfilled.

Of course, when you're waiting passively for something to occur—for your body to become so beautiful that you will achieve all your dreams—it can be a lot more worrisome than something which you do for yourself, and can control. As Ms. de Beauvoir says, when our breasts began to sprout, we had nothing to do with it; they just happened, whether we liked their shape or not. Men followed us with their eyes and commented on our anatomy. We wanted to attract, and yet, in some ways, didn't we all want to be invisible? Surely many of the deep-seated body hang-ups that we now mask with clothing sprang from this feeling of helplessness, this sense we had of being unable to control our changing bodies.

Clothing Has   Society has used clothing very skillfully to establish and to maintain
Kept Us in   woman's traditional role. The dressing of woman as ornament and
Traditional Roles   sexual chattel begins early in life and explains the often quite seductive dress of little girls. In the beginning, the father owns the prize; later, the husband owns it. (The reason, of course, that man has had to "possess" and control woman is elemental—and biological. Making certain of her chastity, and later her constancy, has been the only way he could prove paternity of his children.) If we were to be possessions, man wanted us to be attractive, so that he would be envied by other men. Up until a few years ago, a little girl was physically restricted by her clothing in a way that was needlessly repressive. She was dressed in an extremely short skirt so that she would be appealing and alluring, and then told that she must not let her underpants show. So little girls learned to "scootch down" to pick up the stones in a hopscotch game. They could forget about cartwheels or climbing trees and about almost everything that was physical and fun. This is the woman who now always has to be helped over a fence, who can't possibly teach her kids how to shinny up a tree. It's another price that she's paid for being a female. Her body is not her friend, it's alien to her because it does not move as she wants it to.

Toward a More Honest   In those days when we were growing up, there was a basic con-
Expression of Self and Sexuality   tradiction between our normal, healthy aspirations as human beings

50

and our roles as women. We were told, says Erica Jong, that "our charm lay in weakness. Yet in order to survive, we had to be strong. We were told we were by nature indecisive, yet our very existence often seemed to depend on our decisiveness." We've had to depend on strategy and we've had to manipulate men to get what we want. Female clothing has been an important part of that scheme, and it has been used by women *in all the wrong ways* to seduce, to tease, to pretend an ardor we often did not feel. There's no reason we can't change this calculated quality to a more honest expression of self and sexuality.

In the past, most of a woman's wardrobe was paid for by men, and she had to worry first about what her sponsor—her parent, husband, boss, lover—thought of how she looked in a garment. How she felt in her clothing was often of secondary importance.

Husbands want their wives to look delicious and exciting, but they also want their clothing to say: "She belongs to me. This is my wife, Patricia. Isn't she beautiful? Don't touch!" It's a complicated message, and over the years it's probably confused women's articulation through clothing more than anything else. Her husband wants her to look sexy to impress his friends. She realizes she's on display. She doesn't want to be too attractive to another man (or is worried about what may happen if she is). She is embarrassed at emphasizing her sexuality but doesn't want to miss out on the attention, and she wants sincerely to please her man. She's pulled in all directions.

"Isn't My Wife Beautiful? Don't Touch!"

The women's movement has at last helped the female to feel she has the right to a sense of identity that's all her own, and women seem to have far more confidence now than they had even five years ago about selecting clothing to reflect that identity. Having been dressed quite long enough as a doctor's wife, as a prominent citizen's daughter or even as a rock musician's girl friend, it's time the female paid attention to being herself.

In order to equip herself for new roles, the woman of today needs to sharpen and refine her handling of the clothing language. As in the case of other skills, she has some catching up to do.

Success in a career poses for us a fundamental issue that does not arise for a man, whose human fulfillment and masculine fulfillment are

We're Expected to Excel in Every Role

one and the same. If a man is successful in his profession, he can be a mediocre husband, an inadequate father, an indifferent lover, and he'll have society's approval. But if a woman is active professionally, and also married, she had better be a fantastic wife, a super mom, a gracious hostess and a great lover. She's expected to excel in every role, or she will be condemned for attempting too many. Often the thought of juggling roles boggles her mind and holds the woman back from success. When success comes to a man, it only confirms his sexual image. When it comes to a woman, it threatens hers.

The Female Professional   For the woman who's bridging several worlds, who's functioning in a professional role and fulfilling the duties of female partner and mother as well, there's also the problem of style confusion. Women must pick clothing that will carry them through several roles, sometimes in the course of a few minutes. With these demands, it's complicated and difficult to achieve a consistent sense of style.

When we say that a man's clothing makes him look good, we're really saying that it makes him look authoritative, powerful, rich, responsible, reliable, friendly, masculine. But how does a woman dress to look authoritative, decisive and yet soft and delectably feminine? Sometimes, a friend tells me, she thinks it would be easier to divide herself vertically. "The left shoe could be a sturdy Oxford," she jokes, "and the right one a sexy, high-heeled sandal."

Establishing Rank and Combating Sexual Discrimination   The female wanting to advance in her career treads a narrow path, indeed. Even a slight error in a clothing message can be disastrous. The subtle demonstration of rank is a skill most of the newer female executives have yet to learn. Since the woman executive is generally less accustomed to exercising authority than the male, she tends to be inconsistent and too conscious of herself. That insecurity often makes her go too far in asserting her prerogatives and then retreat uncertainly. So it's important that at least her clothing message be as consistent as possible, that it say to her, as well as to others, that she and her position require respect. When you're bridging gaps in role expectation, remember the importance of manner and demeanor. Dress distinctively enough to gain respect, and to show your taste level, pleasantly enough to attract the right social interchange, and professionally enough to display the efficient, creative energy that's going to get you that raise.

Just as you can tell who's boss by who has the large, corner suite with the windows, so, also, in most corporate structures you'll find that the boss is the one who's wearing the best tailored, three-piece suit. In a well-cut suit with high heels and a briefcase, the woman lawyer is not going to be mistaken for a secretary or a clerk when she shows up in court.

Be careful, however, not to go overboard with the suited look.

Some women are coming up with original variations on this theme. Remember this is an era of free movement in every sense. One client hurried to me after she overheard employees commenting that "Now she's trying to *look* like a man, too." I helped her soften her look, so she could retain her femininity as well as her efficiency.

I do not believe it's especially pleasing or necessary to appear for work every day in a rigid, and strict uniform. Sure, there are times when the authority of a suit is very useful, but overdone, it loses its impact. A symphony, a painting, and a wardrobe all need contrast to be effective and interesting.

Once you have established your credentials and reputation, you might then begin to use more color and softer fabrics and lines in your dress. You should make use of the privilege of being different, of being a smart, chic female in an essentially male office. "In time," the *New York Times* says, "the purposeful young woman executive will be able to relax enough to wear clothes that are more contemporary in structure and cut, but for now she is dressing strictly in self-defense."

One note for the strictly tailored female: remember that the basic difference between men's and women's clothing is in the cut, so remember that your man-tailored suit doesn't have to look like a man's suit. No matter how severe the fabric you choose, be sure that your suit fits your body in a descriptive and pleasing way. Never try to look like an imitation man!

Establishing rank and combating sexual discrimination lead to many kinds of problems for the businesswoman. Marissa needed to soften an ethnic image so that it would not intimidate by its unfamiliarity, and Mrs. Harrison needed to tone down a social-register chic that was hindering her in her work at a city agency. Another client has to get information from Broadway stars for her drama column; she wants her own image, but she knows she must never appear to outshine her sources.

Carolyn sought my advice when she needed to move into a more glamorous look in order to sell her mural paintings to corporations; those casual corduroys just wouldn't do. The artist who seldom emerges from her solitude tends to be one of the harder clients to help. Clothing is often very unimportant to her, and when she sets out to market her work she may automatically don the same costume each time. Her appearance shows exactly what she's done—dressed to go uptown.

Male clothing messages are still easier to understand than female ones. For a long time, the range of choice in clothing for a man has been more limited. With him, it's quality that counts. To see difference in quality, one looks to the tailoring, the detail in the design and the cut. It's easy to distinguish the distinguished.

There's so much variety, so much choice available in women's clothing, that sending a specific clothing message is just that much more difficult. Status level can be seen in cloth, cut, design or designer's name, across a wide range of different styles, and it's easy to err, in either the sending or receiving of these messages.

Also unlike men, women have sometimes found the transition to expressing higher economic or professional status quite difficult. Men seem eager to make the move to a higher style; women often find it a problem. Out of an ingrained guilt, a woman, even if she's making $50,000 a year, sometimes may stay caught in her bargain mentality. She may buy a great deal more now, but every single item is still bought at a bargain price, or it can't be enjoyed.

Clothing Can Keep You in a "Safe" Place   If you're not aware of its power and don't know how to use it (or don't choose to use it), clothing can slow you down and keep you in a "safe" place. One writer I know, working on her first book, became quite close to her editor, and there was potential for real friendship between the two women. However, because the writer wore jeans almost exclusively, she felt somewhat intimidated and uncomfortable in the presence of the other woman's style, and so she found herself making excuses to avoid moving into the new and unfamiliar social world of the editor. How much has this affected her career? It's hard to know. By not breaking out of her jeans uniform, Beverly has managed to "stay in her place," another case of a woman turning away from her chance for success out of fear and insecurity.

None of these women's insecurities is surprising, considering all the assaults upon their body image and upon their worth and value that women have endured through the years. As one of those women, you ought to give yourself a lot of credit for coming as far as you have toward self-acceptance. We have all been deeply imprinted with a sense of inadequacy which will take time and effort to overcome. But you *can* learn to express, not a sexual role, not another's expectation, but a complete, undiluted, undiminished and exciting you!

Self-Acceptance

5

Finding and Expressing the Inner Self

Clothing Can Do a Lot;
It Can't Do Everything

In this chapter, I'm going to ask you to take a good, hard look at yourself and set your goals. What is it you really want to be? Sophisticated? Demure? Elegant? A jet-setter? And is that realistic? Can dress make the difference? Can clothing make you beautiful, bold, mysterious, fragile, childlike, adored?

Clothing can do a lot—but it can't do everything. Back in junior high school, I felt the adolescent pain of being "different," and wanted so badly to look and act and be just like all the fair-haired American girls I knew. I would stare at myself in the mirror, covering the lower half of my face, and try to laugh and speak with my eyes like Grace Kelly. But my eyes were small and dark and never had any of her expression, and I was convinced I must be the homeliest thing in the whole world. Still, I kept trying. I thought by dressing like my idols I could become like them; each day I would carefully write down what the most popular girl in the class was wearing (thus inadvertently beginning a habit of observation which has been invaluable in my career). Only years later did I realize that I had to evolve my own style—I would never be that blonde, blue-eyed American!

When I first conceived of the idea of a consulting service, I knew that mine had to be different. It was not going to be just a shopping service, but also a way of helping a woman with her *inner* as well as her *outer* qualities. Often clients come to me when they want to find or strengthen their own identities, beginning with their clothing image and working inward from there. A widow looking for a new life . . . a woman who feels fed up with being too "bland" all her life . . . the daughter of a famous personality hoping to find her own distinct identity . . . I've seen remarkable changes take place in people who first find out how to express themselves artistically—and then find themselves. This phenomenon is something like what teenagers are about when they experiment with different clothing or hairstyles or even affect a new handwriting. They're hoping to find a style which will say, "Yes, that's me." When their style matches their personality, others react with approval, and that affirmation helps in the identity search.

One of my clients is a handsome, middle-aged woman who had a distinct problem with a double image. Married to one of the country's leading investment bankers, she felt an identity with her husband's world. But, at the same time, she's an accomplished and successful sculptor. When Elizabeth tried to bridge these two lives, she managed to achieve a look which was distinctly neither one—a non-style. Then she tried for a while to maintain two totally separate identities, two wardrobes. But, with the added complication of living in two different cities, and carrying these separate identities around on airplanes to attend a banker's convention one week and a gathering of avant-garde artists the next, this client began to feel, in her own words, "just a little schizie." What she didn't realize was that she didn't have to choose between two worlds; she had to find her own style. Three years later, Elizabeth has a very different appearance. Her style is clear because her identity has been clarified, and her image now comfortably spans both worlds.

Finding personal style means coming to grips with who you really are. And that's not just who you happen to be at age twenty-five or fifty, but who the unchanging person is inside. *A valid personal signature is one that lasts an entire lifetime.* Recognize and rejoice in the fact that you are unique. There's a thread of self-identity that runs through the fabric of our lives; it's a matter of finding it, defining it as style and then adapting the style to our age.

Have you ever looked at an old photograph of yourself and said, "Wow! I was a whole other person then!" Well, were you? Allow yourself, as I did recently, the luxury of spending an afternoon looking back over your life. In old pictures, you can generally see that coalescent quality that runs through your life. Remember how you felt when the pictures were taken—the one when you were nine, standing with your brothers or sisters, or that awkward pose for the snapshots of the senior class. Read the letters and poems that a starry-eyed little girl wrote when she was fifteen. Get in touch with her, and I think you'll discover that that little girl was who you are now. You're not a twenty-five-year-old or a forty-year-old about-to-be-grandmother; you're Ellen or Mary or Joan throughout your life. Get hold of that strong sense of identity and forget about linear time for a while. At different ages, the theme which is you is played at different tempos, it's true, but the *you* which transcends time and body and physical condition is the one that you want to express through your clothing.

When I was a little girl, I was lanky and too tall. I slouched a lot and thought of myself as being weak. People who know me now find it hard to believe that image remains a part of my present self. But in a crisis situation, when I'm most vulnerable, I often revert to that six-year-old feeling. I see the image in old photographs; I hear it, and feel it still within myself, so in my dress I compensate for it—and that helps!

The "Little Waif" Within You

One businesswoman expresses this quality as "the little waif" within her. She had the courage to leave secretarial work years ago to make it big in big business, but often, even now, when she's making a speech or trying to sell a new campaign, the "little waif" portion of her personality comes to the forefront. She counts on her clothing presentation to help her over these hurdles. *When you're insecure inside, you need all the outer cues to be positive.*

"Look Good, But Don't Spend Time on It"

Most people basically do have an innate sense of what looks good on them and what looks awful. They need only to be able to make the commitment to themselves to look good. It became clear to me very

quickly that my client Marian had deliberately turned her back on style. She was the kind whose customary work attire was grass-green synthetic suits, bought somewhere at bargain prices. But, after spending one day with me, she had quickly picked up a level of style so sophisticated that I knew it was impossible I could have taught it all to her in that one day; she'd had the potential all along and just hadn't chosen to use it. She's had a makeup lesson, and her hair restyled. She coordinates and wears her new wardrobe very well and I've never seen her slough off since. Marian told me that when she was a child, she was taught that clothes must never be considered to be important, that she would not be taken as a thinking individual if she spent much time or money on them. "Do look good, but don't spend any time at it," her parents taught her. It took breaking out of that programmed attitude for her to become one of the most attractive travel agents in town. Knowing that she looks good changed the drudgery of her job to hours of pleasurable involvement with others. Instead of leaving her taste and personality at home, she now takes them with her when she goes to work—and the travel business has improved!

Stuck in One Period of Our Lives

We've all seen the person who seems to get stuck in one period of her life and forever after stagnates in the clothing and the hairdo that she wore at that time. Perhaps it was when she was a cheerleader in college; it may not even have been the happiest time of her life, but apparently it was when she felt most in touch with her own identity. And she fears that if she loses that identity she won't have any left at all. Many people who feel this way are able to maintain a false illusion—unfortunately only to themselves—through their dress. When the case is a mild one, we simply think that the person is a bit odd. When it goes too far, we stare at them on the street and call them crazy.

The man whose wife still dresses like that coed cheerleader may never tell her how he feels about her clothes, but he's long since outgrown his college sweetheart. She's still as attractive and exuberant as ever, but the pleated skirts and crew-neck sweaters are simply not appropriate. Struggling to maintain the identity that her husband first loved, she's blind to his unhappiness about the way she looks now.

Stereotyping Ourselves

At the other extreme is the woman who images herself according to her chronological age, rather than to her basic personality. Her dress

59

reflects this. She'll always select the featureless uniform "appropriate" to her age. Accepting herself as a stereotype, she *becomes* the standard, middle-aged lady in a pastel, polyester pants suit, the elderly woman in a dark, print silk dress or the young matron in a dull, cotton shirtwaist. Perhaps she always saw her mother dress in a particular way, so that that way of dressing now signifies respectable adulthood to her. This is the woman who makes an abrupt change in her manner of dress from girlhood to womanhood. And she may feel an obligation to make a clearly defined change in her style when her thirtieth birthday rolls around. But you don't have to stub your toe on those milestones. *When you discover that the essential person within does not change with time, and when you can proudly identify with that inner self, then you will find it easy and natural to dress in harmony with both your age and your personality.*

Comments Vs. Compliments

How do others see you? One way to know is by listening to what they say. Have you heard any of these lately? "I'm ashamed to take you anywhere." "Why can't you look like the other mothers?" "Go get yourself something decent to wear." Or, "Ms. Jones, I feel your attire is distracting to the other people in the office."

Sort these comments out. Differentiate between those that have validity and those that are based on personal prejudice, or even female competitiveness. (Some competitors do a number on you by flicking lint off your coat or pulling a hair from your sweater. If a friend is doing it to be helpful, fine. But if your mother does it to you before she even says hello, it does get annoying.) Beware of the overly helpful, the too specific. Remember that you want guidance in being yourself, not in being someone else's preconceived notion of you.

Perhaps even more important than spoken criticisms are the hidden kind. Because of your dress, you may not be getting promotions at work, your husband may have lost sexual interest, the women you'd like to be friends with may not welcome you, you may be missing out on all kinds of opportunities. Think about it. Could any of this be true in your case?

Take a Loving Survey of Yourself

I'd like you to go to a full-length mirror now. Take this book with you, but don't stop to fix anything. Don't comb your hair, pull down your skirt or put on lipstick. If you're slouching, continue to slouch. Just go and take a good, long, critical, but loving survey of yourself from head to toe, and ask yourself whom you're seeing. Remove yourself. Don't focus into your own eyes and don't look at detail—your hips, or waist or bust—but look at yourself as a total entity. Try to see yourself as others see you. It's hard to do.

"Here," you may say, "is a thirty-year-old with such a happy smile, but in such drab colors." Or, "Here is a woman who carries herself with great dignity. Her facial features are irregular, but striking." Or, "Here is a forty-year-old woman who looks perhaps less than her years. She's slightly plump, but with pleasing proportions."

Many of the things you see as flaws can easily be disguised or deemphasized. Acceptance of yourself doesn't have to mean resignation to what is manifest in reality. A very real part of you is your fantasies, and your fantasies can help you to make yourself what you want to be.

Did you know that the best models aren't really beautiful? That is, they weren't pretty to begin with. Models are tall, and as young teenagers they were usually the ones who grew too fast and felt gawky, so they've had to work hard from the start at acquiring their style. How often I've seen them at the beginning of their careers, like lanky, awkward colts as they come for their first advice on what to wear for their "go-sees" to photographers. These fresh, skinny, unsophisticated kids grow up fast. They work at analyzing themselves, at learning to emphasize their best assets and deemphasize their less-than-perfect parts. There was even one very successful model I knew who had one leg that was shorter than the other. She used to hide it by tilting a little over to the side—the epitome of the art of illusion. *Models Aren't Really Beautiful*

The model knows what attitude and stance can do for an outfit. She knows how looseness gives the look of ease and leanness, and how motion gives an outfit grace. These tricks can be learned through observation and experiment, and you can make them work for you. Anything we can garner from the model is fair game, for it's her "perfection" that is the cause of much of our neurosis about how we look. I've often had the experience of walking into a client's house and being asked, over and over, how much do I weigh, how tall am I, and how can that be? The client can't believe that she might weigh less than I do when she feels so much larger. It's all illusion. *The Art of Illusion*

An executive at a top New York model agency says that when five equally pretty beginner models go for the same job, the one who will get the job is the one who has her own style and projects her own self-confidence. There are lots of pretty faces, so the one who has a sense of herself is always ahead of the game.

When you work with top models as long and as closely as I did—people like Lauren Hutton, Jennifer O'Neill and Twiggy—you learn that the very best models are the ones who are relatively free of personal hang-ups, they are just people who have a sense of themselves. It's the way they feel about themselves that influences how they are treated and how they look in the final printed photographs. That was what convinced me that personal style, developed and earned through internal growth and confidence, is far more valuable than the beauty one just happens to acquire at birth.

Vocabulary and Grammar of the Clothing Language

Now it's time to begin to get down to specifics. You know the importance of the clothing language in your life and you know what you want to project. But, in order to speak your message with clarity, it's necessary to have a knowledge not only of the "alphabet," but of the construction and vocabulary of the language. You need to be aware of your special body problems or other requirements of your life situation; you need to train your eye to pick out what's good and what's bad for you. You'll want to be knowledgeable about the qualities of various colors and fabrics; and to complete your new image you'll probably need an ability to get good value for your dollar.

In this chapter, some of these basic lessons will be covered. Let's start with the principle of providing focus in your dress.

The Focal Point

You should direct the observer's eye to where you want it to go. Just as there's a focal point in every good photograph or painting, so should there be one point of emphasis in every ensemble you create. As a matter of fact, it's disturbing to the observer if there is none. A planned focal point should be inherent in the structure of your dress every day.

If your waistline is small and your midriff is good, your focal point could be a wide cummerbund or a good-looking belt buckle. Earrings or makeup or a ruffled neck blouse can move the focus to your face. A skirt with a slit or a high-heeled shoe can place the focal point at your leg.

Don't, however, put all of your focus on a good feature if, by doing so, you expose a poor feature. If you have small, pretty feet but are big in your build, don't choose dainty, cut-out sandals with high heels. Everyone will be watching every step that you take in fear for your safety, and your extra weight will be much more evident than if you choose a firmer foundation to walk on.

Use focal points to draw attention away from figure flaws. Jewelry against a dark dress can draw attention away from the figure, though jewelry against a *light* background will call attention to it. Over and over again in this book, I'll stress the fact that layered clothing is a godsend. It can help to normalize almost all figure types. A vest, a jacket, a sweater, a shawl—all of these things draw interest and give flair and dash; they disguise but at the same time, by completing an outfit, they give it more importance and a pulled-together look that is both chic and casual.

Often the way you feel about yourself is the message that comes across. If you walk into a party thinking of your hips, how big they are, you call people's attention to those hips through your self-conscious posture and awkwardness. The flaw you're trying most to hide becomes the inevitable focus. There's an energy in concentration that attracts attention. If you resolve not to worry about a problem, the chances are your easygoing manner will be transmitted and the problem will attract virtually no attention at all.

The second important principle of dress is balance. All of us have *Balance* qualities we like and features we dislike. Often you can *balance* a body or a personality type by dressing slightly against it. Balance big hips with unskimpy tops, short legs with jackets which are not too long. If you have a soft body, wear clothes with structure that suggest energy and efficiency; if your body is muscular, use softer fabrics and lines. If your manner is usually passive, pick clothes that project with pleasant colors and crisp tailoring.

If you have an aggressive nature, choose gentler lines and colors. If you tend to be a little frantic, always on the go, it doesn't make sense to wear clothing that could be considered overbearing. Wear vibrant colors if these are best for you, but try to select solids, for example, and not eye-dazzling prints. Or, if you wear a busy print, opt for muted colors on a small scale.

The shy person can help herself by wearing up-to-date clothes. Not necessarily the very latest or a fad, but definitely not something conspicuously out-of-date, for that draws unwanted attention. Pleasant colors are often the best way to transmit the message that you're approachable.

Often the obese woman who is not proud of her body places her equity on beautiful hair, nails and jewelry. She learns exquisite taste and skill in makeup. It's her way of balancing her assets, of keeping up her morale, and I say bravo to that!

The assets you wish to highlight might include your beautiful eye or hair color, but don't be too obvious about it. Don't buy all blue clothing if you have blue eyes, or all green with your red hair. It's trite. Remember, you want people to notice that you look good, not just that you have good matching ability.

If your figure is attractive, let it show, but don't make every outfit a total inventory of your physical assets. Overexposure of even your best points is self-defeating. And never be too serious in your dress. An amusing note is okay. Pauline Trigère would sometimes pin her elegant turtle pin to the hem of her dress. Take something elegant and make it whimsical.

"What Can I Do About My Age?"

Some clients have remarked that "What you say is all very well. I can dress in harmony with my personality, I can camouflage or correct my body flaws, but what can I do about my age?"

The best approach, of course, is not to be ashamed of healthy age. For each tiny line, you've probably learned a hundred things you never understood when you were younger. Appreciate your age and the extra charm and wisdom it can give you, and don't assume that your body has to look bad just because you're getting older.

There are some specific tricks to flatter the woman who is maturing. You should wear pretty colors next to your face. Use an off tint of your clothing color as your eye-shadow color (very lightly, please). Generally, you should be wearing better-quality garments as you mature, with perhaps fewer pieces, parts and complications. Be careful not to clang around with too much jewelry. And no fads—nothing that looks like a desperate lunge for youth and chic. It's during adolescence that we dress primarily for the reaction of others; at maturity, after full integration of the personality, one can dress primarily for oneself.

If your body is younger than your face, do draw attention to your figure. Try to remember your sense of youthful movement to improve your walk. In clothing, anything formal or rigid always has an aging effect, so go for ease and simplicity. Never dress as if you're sitting for your portrait. And remember, you've worked hard for maturity, so enjoy it!

Getting Out of a Rut

Don't cling stubbornly to a particular clothing style to the exclusion of others unless you really know what you're missing. Sometimes a client feels she looks skinnier and sleeker in a narrow, straight skirt. I urge her to vary the look once in a while with the easy, graceful swing of a flair skirt, particularly if the longer length is flattering to the proportions of her body. There's nothing like a longer full skirt for femininity.

A diminutive woman teetering along the street in four-inch heels does, indeed, look taller, but does she have any idea what she has sacrificed? Does she know that she's given up grace? In the same way that enhancing a good feature can point up a bad, by covering one body flaw you may be creating another unattractive feature in posture or movement. Sometimes it's best to leave well enough alone.

All those familiar old favorites that have become like a security blanket to you may not be just protecting you from the world—perhaps they're also *keeping* you from it. So wait a minute! Before you put on that shirtwaist dress again, before you wear the same skirt with the same shirt with the same shoes, think about it. When people find a clothing formula that clicks, they frequently work it to death.

Try Something New

"I'd feel downright silly wearing that flowery thing." If you believe you're the geometric, tailored type, and you go for stripes or foulards or checks rather than flowery prints, fine. But next time try buying your geometric prints in a collarless drawstring blouse, rather than a classic shirt-collar top. Or try a coordinated, small geometric-print scarf inside another geometric-print shirt collar. Have you ever worn tweeds and small geometrics together? They often make beautiful and interesting combinations.

If you're a more fragile type, you probably like floral prints, but be creative about your look. Try reversing the reasoning above. Floral beauties are expected to be swathed in bows and ruffles, low-plunging necklines and full-skirted dresses. Don't always go for the bow just because that's what's expected of you. Try the same floral print in a very tailored look. Perhaps your old standby soft floral blouse could be worn under a strict suit.

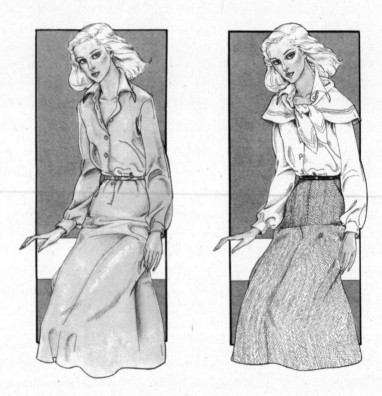

If you've always worn a shirtdress, and feel most comfortable attired that way, why don't you try a shirt and classic skirt, a belt and little neckerchief, for a change? Or put a patterned sweater vest over the blouse and a little belt on top of the vest, to be worn outside of the skirt. The shirtdress wearer should feel comfortable in both these changes.

Get rid of old definitions in your wardrobe. Instead of that "spring coat," allow yourself to think of a soft wool shawl, or a day-to-evening black, shiny raincoat. Instead of the usual ascoted blouse under your black velvet dinner suit, how about a bare silk camisole? And never automatically say, "Oh, no, that's not for me." Allow yourself a frill once in a while, even when you don't "deserve" it. If you've had the dream of a white blazer all your life, don't let a sticky-fingered toddler stand in the way. Particularly if that "toddler" is ten years old now.

If a pants suit fits your life-style so well it's become your uniform, surprise people by showing up in a dress once in a while. Perhaps the dress for you isn't a flounced floral, but a covered sweater dress might be just right. Find your own adaptation of the style.

A successful woman lawyer I know almost always wears three-piece tweed suits with low-heeled, comfortable shoes. But, once in a while, she shows up in the courtroom in a floral skirt, silky blouse and graceful, sling-back heels. It's still a businesslike look, but it's enough of a change to give her a lift—and the judge and jury seem to appreciate it, too.

What does color say about you? The psychologist Max Luscher has done some extraordinary work in projecting a person's entire personality profile merely by asking him or her to list eight color samples in order of preference. When I choose colors for a client, generally her coloring, complexion and hair determines which color *family* I select, but her personality determines the *intensity* of that color. *What Does Color Say About You?*

I believe that color can be immensely important in setting style and mood. Most people who tend to favor one color do so not because it's their perfect signature, but because they're too lazy to experiment with other colors and combinations. I'm not talking about the very few fashion experts who achieve an effective look with all black, or chic beige or all off-white—it's a rare woman who can get away with that kind of advanced fashion look. So don't be a monochrome. If you find yourself locked into just one or two colors, challenge your habit. Once in a while, try a pattern introducing a color that you're not used to, even if it's only a scarf or a little vest. Wearing a different color is a sure way to create some excitement.

Balancing Color   Ideally, one should wear a balance of lights and darks, solids and prints; vibrant colors are sometimes prettiest in "just a peek"—a pencil-yellow scarf, for instance, inside the shirt neckline whose print just picks up that color. Dressing in solid colors is easiest, but buy an occasional print for accent. Find the colors that make you feel best, that make you glow. Some faces come alive when surrounded by clear, bright color; others become washed out and need softer color help. It wouldn't hurt to spend a few minutes in front of a mirror with good light, systematically checking colors against your face. File away what you learn for future reference.

Exposing light skin at the neckline to achieve that light-dark balance

To show creativity, one doesn't always have to experiment with a new silhouette. Often a familiar style in a brand-new color will serve the same purpose. Each season the fashion industry pushes a group of new colors. Usually they do look refreshingly new, and there's normally a large selection of fashions to choose from in those particular colors. Its wide availability makes the new color more comfortably familiar, and yet it's still new enough to desire.

Here are some more hints on creativity with color. By putting a different combination of colors together, you can often come up with a totally different effect. Try burgundy and rust, or electric blue and lacquer red, or jade green and pale banana yellow. They evoke different responses, don't they?

In a two-color outfit, the balance is generally more pleasing when the darker color is worn on the bottom. If you're wearing a cream colored skirt with a black silk blouse, I'd like to see some balance of that lighter cream color on top–a silk flower, a cream neck scarf with a print of tiny black pin-dots, or a matching cream jacket. Exposing light skin at the neckline is another way to achieve that light-dark balance.

A neck scarf in the same shade as the skirt will tie your outfit together

*Balancing too printy a look with a
solid color at the neck*

If you are wearing a solid-color skirt with a print blouse, a turtleneck
or neck scarf in the same shade as the skirt will bring the color of the
skirt up and tie your outfit together (even when the print does not
include that color).

When you wear a bright, outstanding color or print, the line of your
outfit should be simpler, to compensate for the drama of the color. If
you want to wear your bright print skirt with a coordinated print
blouse—but on you it looks too printy—try balancing with touches of
solid color (one of the colors in the print), at the neck with a
turtleneck or just a dickey, or at the waist with a solid-color belt or
solid scarf tied around to give a cummerbund effect.

If your outfit is too solid, counter with a third layer in a print blouse, perhaps folded up in back, tied in a square knot in front and left unbuttoned. It will have the effect of a casual blouson jacket. In the summer you could wear a colorful cotton stripe over a solid skirt and blouse of the two primary colors in the stripe.

Always remember to balance the weight of the fabric against the intensity of the color. Red, for example, is not a very good color for me; I feel garish and overdone in it. But when I'm asked to wear red for television, I can make it work by choosing a sheer, airy fabric which immediately diffuses the intensity of the color.

The possibilities for changing your mood or enhancing your image through color never end. Don't be afraid to experiment.

There are two distinctly different principles that you can employ in planning your new image. The purchases you make for your wardrobe will depend on whether you're a *traditionalist* or a *fashion follower.* Think about which pattern of dress suits you best.

The fashion-conscious woman picks clothes for their excitement and fun, rather than for long-term, enduring value. She usually has the ability to design her wardrobe so that she gets a great deal of creative use from her clothes, in terms of both fashion and money.

The traditionalist is generally not as fond of shopping as the trendy woman. She makes fewer shopping trips and buys classics that carry her through several years. She knows quality. Her wardrobe generally revolves around a few basic colors, perhaps taupe, mahogany, beige or black. She expects an outfit to serve for more than one season and for more than one role. She adds color and spice in small touches, and she updates her wardrobe only occasionally with accessories.

The traditionalist approach is a more thought-out, European way of dressing, and it may be slightly more economical in the long run. The traditionalist's statement reflects her sense of long-term good taste in a muted, quiet way.

A typical core winter wardrobe of quality for the traditionalist, costing about $500, would be something like the following: one tweed flare skirt ($70), one silk blouse ($50), one well-tailored wool blazer ($120), one wool pants suit with matching shirt-jacket and pant ($130), and one classic khaki raincoat ($130).

The trend-lover's clothing language message is her creativity, her excitement, her fashion-consciousness.

For the same amount, the follower of the latest fashions would include in her winter wardrobe: one native (i.e., Aztec-textured) wrap jacket ($60), one 7/8 length sweater jacket ($40), one long, ethnic midi-skirt ($45), a lacy Victorian blouse ($35), one long, tweed midi-skirt ($45), a suede jerkin ($30), three great colored sweaters ($75), a pair of pants ($45), a cossack blouse ($25), a peasant floor-length skirt ($50) and a dramatic shawl ($50).

Which are you? Which would you rather be? Don't assume your

type on the basis of past behavior. You may think you're a traditionalist, but are you really? Or was it just parental training? Remember, this is a chance for a new you. Maybe you'd have more fun creating lots of different looks, and keeping up-to-the-minute. Or have you been racing to keep up when you really don't like shopping that much? Perhaps you'd like to settle into quality garments that you could wear for years.

If you're just starting, the traditionalist's way will be a bit easier until your eye is developed enough to know which style is you, until you know which stores to run into for the odd piece of clothing that you need to complete an outfit. Also, tailored clothes tend to look good on more people. It's that almost universally flattering look of tailored clothing that's the reason the most successful manufacturers today are those in sportswear separates.

Remember, whichever path you choose, that you can't save money on some items—on cheap shoes, on poor-quality bags or on a badly tailored jacket.

For beginners at any skill or sport, there are always rules to make it easier. Make a decision to follow one of these two patterns. Later on, when you're a pro, you can begin to flout some of the basic principles and get away with it; for now, take things one step at a time.

One Step
at a Time

If a woman is not ready for the status that her clothing proclaims, then the clothing easily wears the woman. The irony is that a person's fears, self-doubts and inadequacies are never so apparent as when she is attempting frantically to be something she is not. Sometimes a client will try to move too quickly toward her desired image of herself. She'll dress beyond her role, become lost and slip back several steps. Dress just one step above where you are now, but let it be comfortable. Give yourself time to integrate each level of sophistication. Then, by enhancing your look slightly, and by feeding on the approval of others to increase your self-confidence, you'll soon be ready to take another step forward.

Let's take as an example a woman who comes to me in a double-knit, brown blazer jacket and pants outfit with a basic white polyester blouse. The first step would be to take her out of matching sets and put her into a more sophisticated fabric and color. A brown tweed, for instance, mixed with brown solid creates a much more youthful and stylish look. Now let's get her out of always wearing pants. Since she's got the tweed jacket, we'll buy her a dark, solid skirt and begin to teach her about accenting with color, with a print blouse that will pick up the color of the new skirt. We could continue by having her try wearing the tweed blazer over a traditional evening fabric, like a lovely, deep-wine velvet skirt. How much more creative and interesting the combined textures are than a solid velvet skirt with a solid velvet jacket that matches!

This lady has come a long way already. Her ability to mix and match (and unmatch) represents a new level of understanding. She's learned a separates look. Instead of always relying on pants, she's coordinating separate tops and skirts into her formerly dull wardrobe and beginning to evolve a look of her own.

Now, assuming my client wants to go further, we take her the next step. I see that her present wardrobe is quite sporty, and I want to get her into a few softer dresses; say, two-piece dresses, perhaps with a shawl, so she can wear the top of her dress as a blouse, with her new shawl, over pants and skirts already in her wardrobe. With new-found confidence, she'll be bound by fewer "rules." She can wear the tweed blazer over her new dresses if they are solid or small geometric prints. She might even get to a level where she feels comfortable casually draping the solid shawl over her blazer! It takes some practice to use these tricks effectively, but it does get to be fun.

Try This On for Size   Here are a few exercises to help you get rid of your musty old misconceptions about your clothing message. Don't try them all at once, please; take your time, and learn to enjoy and appreciate your new skills.

1. For one week, try to project a different image each day, and observe the reactions of others. Every evening, decide whether that new image has had an effect on the events of the day or on your mood.

2. See if you can vary one outfit with accessories three different ways—different enough so you won't mind wearing that same basic dress.

3. If you tend to wear one color, try staying away from it totally for one whole week. Did you miss it?

4. If you wear heavy makeup, try less. If you don't wear makeup, try a little. Experiment.

5. Try concentrating on new ideas for your hair.

6. Try consciously to get three genuine compliments on your appearance.

It's really all a matter of becoming at ease with style. Getting your look together is being prepared for the game that's played out there in the world. When you are prepared, playing that game can be a pleasure.

6
Your Body

A Profile of
Your Proportions   Thanks to that wondrous invention, clothing, most of our physical defects can be artfully concealed—or at least minimized—with a few simple tricks. But first it's important to know what exactly the problems are. In the last chapter, we talked about what you thought about your body. Now let's forget about feelings and phobias and get down to facts and inches. You'll need a measuring tape for this, and it's best to take measurements in the undergarments that you normally wear. What we're after is a profile of your proportions, which can be tremendously helpful in learning to achieve the most flattering look.

Know the Facts,
Then Produce the Illusion   First, do you have big bones or small? If you're small-boned, your wrist will measure less than six inches; over six inches, you're relatively large-boned, and your best weight, of course, would be higher.

If you're short-waisted, that's not just a problem to be dealt with above the waist. It may also mean, if other measurements are normal, that your lower torso or legs are particularly long, which may call for some adjustments in the clothing you buy and wear.

In the ideally proportioned figure, half of the length of the body is above the hip and half below, with the lower half evenly divided by the

76

knees. Also, shoulders should measure the same number of inches across as the measurement from the nape of the neck to the back of the waist. Thus, the top of the body should, ideally, be a perfect T. Your posture and good shoulders are most important, because well-cut clothing is made to be carried on the shoulders. Any dressmaker will tell you that a woman's best asset is a good pair of shoulders.

How long are your arms? Your elbows should normally fall at the waist and your fingertips at midthigh. My elbow is two inches below my waist, and, sure enough, every sleeve length is the same two inches short.

Now let's compare the rest of your measurements to the normal American standard. In determining your own statistics, do try to resist the temptation to pull in a little tighter at the hips and waist. Don't cheat. Realize that you have to know the facts in order to produce the illusion. Just relax and have faith.

Chart of Standard Body Proportions

Height	Shoulder Width	Back from Nape of Neck
under 5′2″	14½″	14½″
5′2″–5′4″	15″	15″
5′4″–5′6″	15½″	15½″
5′6″–5′8″	16″	16″
5′8″–5′10″	17″	17″
5′10″–6′	17½″	17½″

Dress Size	Bust	Waist	Hips
4	32	23	35
6	33	24½	36
8	34	26	37
10	34–36	27½	38
12	36	29	39
14	38	30½	40
16	40	32	41

Specific Figure Types and How to Deal With Them

Now that your measurements are recorded, I bet things weren't as bad as you thought. Keep in mind that these are standards for so-called ideal proportions, not averages. A large proportion of American women are shortwaisted, and a great many women have heavy upper thighs. Probably the most common American figure has hips at least one size larger in a skirt, and two sizes larger in pants, than in a blouse. About half of all women are round in the torso, while others' shapes are wider but flatter. Figures are not ideal. What we want to do is work with the body you have, and make it look its absolute best.

Now have the courage to study yourself nude in front of the mirror. Face up to each of your figure flaws. In self-examination, many people tend to extremes, either blinding themselves to their faults or seeing nothing else. Do try to see both good and bad, and give equal emphasis to each. Remember, you are not alone in having something that you wish to conceal. Ninety-eight percent of us (at least!) have something we wish we didn't, or don't have something we wish we did. After several years of watching the top professional models in the world running around in the nude, I know for a fact that they are exactly the same as all the rest of us—only a little skinnier! I wish my clients and friends were aware of that. Often only a few extra pounds keep us from being proud of our shapes. It's one of the less logical quirks of human nature, I think, that many of us spend our lives fretting about the same five pounds. It's like going through life always ten minutes late!

Some women will find that their bodies look better nude than clothed. They have a great and achievable goal—to make their clothes look as good as their bodies! Often, because we don't understand body proportion, we exaggerate our flaws and disguise our best assets.

Now let's talk about some specific figure types, and how to deal with them.

Tall and Thin

If you're tall and thin, first of all, be glad! Clothing just naturally looks great on you. Wear clothing that moves with your body—you're the one who can carry off those beautiful softly textured fabrics, even bulky ones such as rabbit hair and mohair. Let some skin show. Don't cover yourself up with a vast expanse of fabric. Nothing should be too short or skimpy either, from hemline to hair length. Most important of all is a straight, proud carriage.

Thin bodies connote incisiveness and exciting activity. Even the very thin woman can be extremely attractive. She should, however, not wear anything bare or clinging. Fullness and softness are her tricks of illusion. Soft, fluffy wools, fur or, in summer, airy voile and gauze are good choices. Boots are a boon to the thin girl, for they camouflage skinny legs under skirts. Avoid clothing with vertically striped patterns or with proportions that are too long for you, thus pulling the eye straight downward to make you look thinner than you are.

Keep the skinny part that most bothers you under wraps. For instance, your throat may feel too exposed without a scarf, choker, high cowl neck or long hair. If you're too straight ("built like a stick"), establish a waistline by wearing different tones of separates or by wearing a full skirt nipped in with a belt. Prints should not be too prominent or large-scaled (since people will have to walk all the way around you to see the complete pattern). Avoid prissy bows and ruffles; they've been associated with the very thin for far too long and have an unfortunate connotation.

Some pluses for you are blouson waists (tuck in your blouse tightly, then raise your arms to relax the look), soft cowl necklines, fuller, more graceful sleeves, gentle, full skirts. Again, layering adds interest and disguises thinness. Like the very short woman, you should avoid heavy shoes. They'll make your legs look even thinner.

For the Short

If you are short, don't chop up your body with contrasting bold colors. One color or a mix of soft tones is best. Simple dresses and jumpers tend to give you a longer line. Most important for you, no overpowering anything—hats, hair styles or jewelry. You should wear nothing that is big, bulky or complicated. Proportion is the word for you to keep in mind. Never clutter up your neck; that tends to foreshorten your figure.

Many people deny themselves variety in dress because of preconceived ideas and rules, shibboleths that need to be shattered. Some short women, for example, feel they cannot wear a longer-length skirt. Actually, if your body proportions are good, especially if you have "high knees" (that is, if you are long from your knees to your ankles), your height doesn't rule out longer skirts, provided the outfit is scaled down to you. (For a short person, perfect hem length is vital. Too long and too short a skirt are both shorteners.) Sometimes the trick can be to change to a more delicate, high-heeled shoe. High heels are flattering, as long as they are not grotesquely high. That's a mistake many short women make—a mistake because the effort is too obvious and arched, in both senses of the word. Avoid ankle straps or heavy shoes because they will call attention downward and make the leg look shorter. The hose shouldn't draw attention either, for that tends to emphasize the shortness of leg.

To look longer or slimmer, wear a single color or tones of a single-color family, as we've said. Pick a slimmer skirt rather than a full dirndl in a heavy fabric, or choose a skirt with soft gathering at the center

To Look Slimmer

Wrong   Right

front and back (not around the sides if you are hippy). Wear solids or neat prints rather than large, splashy prints, and try vertical patterns or vertical seaming. And stay away from oversized anything—collars, shoulders, bulky layers or pant cuffs—to detract from the vertical line. A shorter jacket gives a leggier appearance.

If you are short and also thin, remember that light colors give importance to a small, slender figure and keep it from fading away.

If You Are Large

If you are large, that's what you are. Heavy frames sometimes have a built-in presence of which one ought to take advantage. Clothing must fit well. It should be comfortably loose except in the shoulder, which is likely to be your narrowest part, where it should be closely fitted. A loose tent isn't the perfect answer because one imagines all sorts of unseen horrors beneath it. On the other hand, of course, don't wear anything skintight. Avoid wearing any large expanse of bold pattern. A well tailored dark suit with a touch of softness and color at the neck will draw the focal point upward toward the face. Avoid front-pleated trousers, or pleated or dirndl skirts. Remember that yards and yards of fabric have the effect of adding pounds and pounds.

Some heavy women do not like to show their arms and always wear long, opaque sleeves. Others want to be seen only in black, navy or brown because they want to hide heaviness. But the color and shape of your clothing is wrong if it calls attention to your problem by being out of season. If you're heavy, it might be better to wear a pretty, flattering color occasionally, rather than always the predictable dark "slimming" shades. Don't hide; use pleasant attraction instead.

Your Body Characteristics: Face and Neck

The woman with the round face will only emphasize her roundness with jewel-necked Peter Pan collars. Don't wear high choker necklaces, which shorten your neck. Hanging necklaces elongate. Your hair style should be short to medium, brushed away from the face, but never in any kind of bowl style. Any V-neck is good—remember that classic shirts should always be worn open down to the second or third button. Wide U-necks are fine, but no high ruffles.

If your face is long, your hair style should be a medium length and

Wrong   Right

should either have lift or fullness to the cut. Sharp V-necks and hanging necklaces are not good, but bows and soft cowls are fine.

Long Face

Wrong   Right

Clients have often told me they can't wear turtlenecks because they have short necks, so they choose instead the "mock" turtleneck line. This is an instance where it should be the real thing or nothing at all. Most mock turtlenecks tend to look provincial; they lack high style. Only if your head sits smack on your shoulders should you give up a real turtleneck; its sleek effect can never be duplicated with a shirt. I think it's worth it to wear one sometimes, even if your neck is not so long as you'd like. Of course, I don't mean an exaggerated, gigantic one.

Short Neck

Wrong

Right

Long Neck

Wrong

Right

If your jacket collar sits slightly away from the neck and is low in the back, your neck will look longer. If you have short hair or wear a chignon, you should let some skin show between hair and collar.

If your neck is too long, it's better not to expose too much of it. (Fashion magazines don't consider long necks a problem, but you may.) Cowlneck sweaters, ruffle and bow blouses, and necklaces to fill in the neckline would be a good idea (but no rigid chokers sitting at the base of your neck to emphasize where one starts measuring upwards). Your hair should be medium to long length.

For a double chin, a long pendant worn low on the chest is usually a good distraction. Stay away from big earrings and avoid high chokers at the throat. Collars should be simple and flat and should rest on your shoulders. Large, stiff collars are no good; they seem to have a life of their own, and they crowd your neck. Big bows, big turtlenecks and high ruffles are no-no's for sure. And, like the woman with the short neck, you can never go wrong with a classic shirt collar open down to the second or third button.

Wide Shoulders

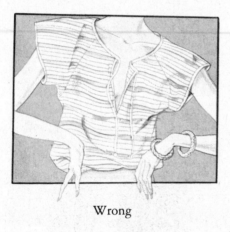 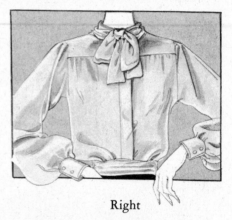

Wrong   Right

Shoulders   If your shoulders are wide, try to avoid cap sleeves or dolman sleeves. Shoulder seams should lie one inch inside your real shoulder line to give the illusion of narrower shoulders. No sleeveless looks or puckering at the shoulder seams or any sort of puff sleeve for you. And softer fabrics are certainly better than stiff or heavy ones across your shoulders.

If your shoulders are too square, you should avoid a straight line across them like a horizontal, striped pattern or a bateau neckline. Silk blouses with gentle gathering at the yoke are certainly the most softening thing to wear. Raglan sleeves are better than boxy, set-in sleeves which emphasize squareness.

Sloping Shoulders

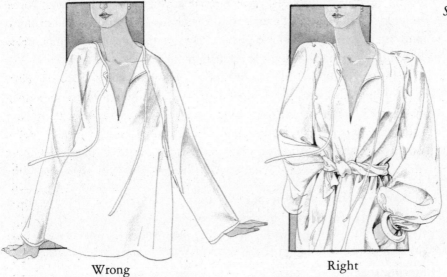

Wrong

Right

Narrow Shoulders

Wrong

Right

For sloping shoulders, the halter neckline, raglan sleeves, collarless styles and big bows or lapels may all be treacherous. Remind yourself to stand up straight, because slumping accentuates the problem. Crisp fabrics and tailored shoulders give the illusion of a good set of natural shoulders underneath.

If you have narrow shoulders, the advice given for those with sloping shoulders will generally hold true for you. Seam lines of your clothing should be at the outer edge of your natural shoulders. Epaulette-type details are fine, but they shouldn't swallow you. Cap sleeves are good. Any sleeves are better for you than a sleeveless line because they disguise with their grace and fullness. Never wear raglan sleeves, which make you look even narrower. Look for tops that have gathering where they are attached to the shoulder line—they're wonderful for you. And crisp fabrics that tailor well are always good.

Bust   Bosom problems are among the more easily remedied figure flaws. Too large or pendulous breasts can be corrected or minimized with the right bra (even if it has to be custom-made). When there's a choice, I'd stick to a no-seam, natural looking bra, never pulled too high (or left too low).

Many women skimp on the time and money they spend on brassieres. Find a fitter who can help you select the correct cup size and the correct overall measurements. Cherish her—bra fitting is a difficult science. I can't stress too much how important a well-fitting bra is. It can make an amazing difference in the way your clothes fit. *You should be sure to be fitted for a bra before you purchase any clothing at all.*

If your bosom is too much of a good thing, lead the eye away with pretty collars, subtly gathered shoulders, or with colors that flatter and draw attention to your face and eyes. Vertical necklines are good. Stay away from big, cowlneck sweaters and clinging, tight tops. Wide belts bring your big bosom even closer to your waist, and double-breasted jackets make you look stiff and heavy. Watch out for horizontal stripes and bulky layering that emphasize width, and avoid light colored tops over dark pants or skirts. Also, keep away from empire waists, which only draw attention to the bosom.

If you have a tiny bust, the shoulders become even more important in the fit. Most small-busted women seem to have good, straight

Wrong   Right

shoulders. Try soft shirring from the shoulder lines, or from yokes, and
pretty, attention-getting details like tucking, gathers, smocking, embroidery and pockets or tabs. Avoid clinging fabrics over the bust.

Wrong   Right

Flowing, big blouse tops in pretty prints distract the eye from the too straight figure and add to the picture of soft femininity. And, of course, you have two choices for the bra to wear beneath; you can get a softly padded one (not too obvious, please), or you can be happily au naturel with the figure that's very much in vogue—or, at least, in *Vogue*!

Heavy Arms

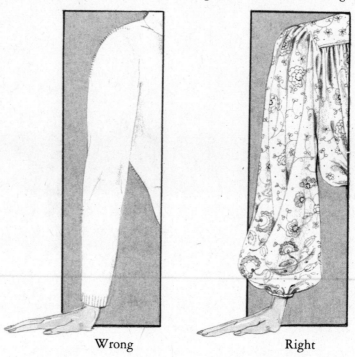

Wrong   Right

Arms   If your arms are heavy or too thin, don't wear clinging fabrics or tight-fitting sleeves.

When heavy arms need to be covered, it sometimes adds a youthful touch to roll up a long sleeve, especially in the summer when others are wearing sleeveless. You won't look obviously out of season even though your arms are covered. Soft, sheer sleeves are flattering to you, too.

Waist   How is your waist? Are you starting to have problems with a midriff bulge that threatens to descend and obliterate your waist completely? Don't despair, but don't go on accentuating the flaw by wearing outfits that change color at the waist. Some may tell you not to wear a belt if you have waist problems, but I think that's sometimes giving up too much. If you have a third-layer shirt or loose jacket covering the sides of your waist, you can still put a belt on underneath to finish the look. You'll only be seeing the front of the belt! A narrow belt for you should probably not be narrower than one inch—so it won't get lost.

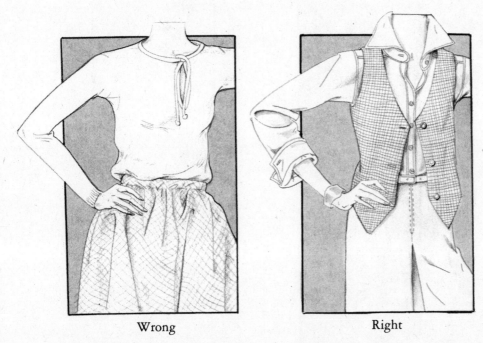

Large Waisted

Wrong

Right

The woman who feels she's "straight up and down"—with no waist visible from the front—sometimes avoids wearing clothing that displays her figure. But she should also remember to look at the side view, which may be very slim and attractive. Some of us rounder types would envy her figure—and there we are again, in that automatic rut of envy. Remember, most people do not see you straight on as you see yourself in the mirror; seventy-five percent of the time, you'll be seen at other angles!

If there's a tendency to short-waistedness, wear tops outside the skirt or pants and cheat by pushing your (narrow) belt down a little lower than your natural waist. If you have to tuck in your top, you should blouse it over the belt for disguise; you gain a half-inch-longer waist.

Alter waistbands to make them narrower, and don't wear wide belts. You might try an authentic empire. It can be a very good line for some. Don't make an abrupt color change at the waist, and, if there is a difference in tone between blouse and skirt, match your belt to the *top's* color for just a little more illusion.

Short Waisted

Wrong

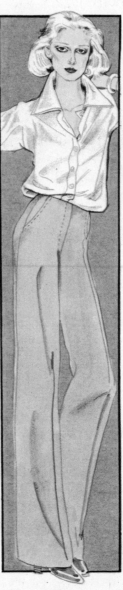

Right

If you're long-waisted, count your blessings. You should be happy about it. You can weigh more without it showing. However, if you want to de-emphasize a long waist, don't wear a skinny sweater top, but rather a softer, more distracting top. Also, match your belt to the *skirt* or *pants* color, instead of to the top. You've got the torso length to wear those great, wide cummerbund belts.

Long Waisted

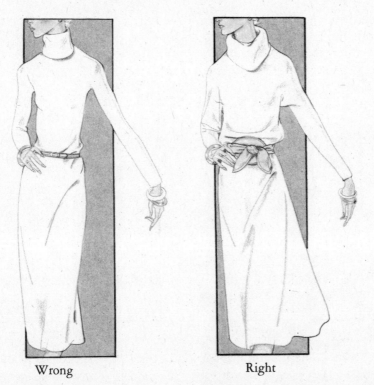

Wrong   Right

Stomach

If you have a bit of a protruding abdomen, steer clear of clingy fabrics and any other fabrics that will hang heavily over the stomach. Wear graceful A-lines—but never bulky dirndls or loose pleats. Sewn-down pleats have a controlling girdle effect. Choose those sewn down to about four to four-and-a-half inches; longer than that just emphasizes the big tummy, because the skirt begins to collapse in underneath. Straight skirts are not good; they tend to cling under the stomach, too, and accentuate the problem. Don't wear your waistbands too snug. It's preferable for the waistline of your dress to be just slightly above your waist, so it doesn't draw attention to the difference between your waist

91

and stomach. An empire waistline looks good, too. Side slash pockets divert the eye from the center of the tummy. Hard-finish fabrics have a neat, slimming effect. Probably best of all is a skirt with gentle little gathers at the sides of the skirt front.

Stomach

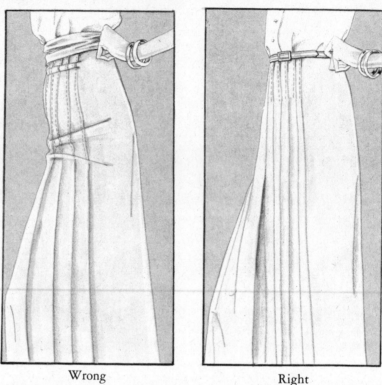

Wrong   Right

Hips   Most women are unhappy about their hips. Hardly anybody has those magical, slim, boyish hips that models seem to display. We all feel too wide.

The hippy woman should avoid straight skirts (and pants unless a top covers part of the hips from the rear). Also avoid pocket detail. If the dressmaker is making you a skirt, a good trick is to add a fake, buttoned placket down the front which draws attention away from the sides of the hips. Pants are not terrific, but, before you give up trousers, try them with a vest or jacket that can be worn casually open but never taken off in public. An attractive top worn outside the pants might offer some security, too. Some hippy women are so anxious for the jackets to cover the whole hip area that they wear them much too long for their leg proportions. Sure, they hide their hips, but for that they pay the price of looking squat. If you are shorter than 5'3" and hippy, don't worry if a jacket doesn't cover your whole hip area; most of the world will be looking at you from above—and from that angle your hips will seem disguised.

For big hips, A-line, and slightly gathered dirndls are best. You don't want the skirt to look puffy, but you do want it to move softly. The amount of fabric at the skirt's hem has to be generous enough to balance your hippiness.

For wide hips and big thighs, no pleated pants or pleated skirts, no back pockets, no big plaids or horizontal patterns. Be wary of back zippers. Bias-cut skirts will cling in the wrong places. And use that third loose layer—jacket or vest or sweater! For heavy "drumstick" thighs, it might help to buy pants one size larger for enough ease in the crotch and fullness in the upper legs. You can then have the waistband taken in, an easy alteration.

Wide Hips

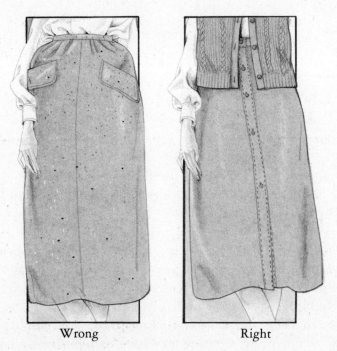

Wrong   Right

If your hips are large in proportion to your waist (twelve or more inches larger than the waistline), the trick, to create an illusion of better proportion, is to conquer the impulse to emphasize that tiny waist, which may be your proudest asset. It may be hard to change a long-standing habit, particularly if you have placed your equity in that small waist, but try wearing a narrower belt that's a little loose, a little lower so that it does not hourglass your figure. Or, if you're not short-waisted and your hips come out like a shelf, wear the waistline slightly above your waist. A-line dresses are always good.

Hourglass Figure

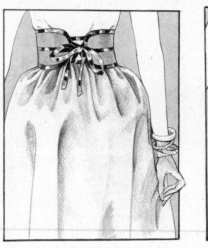 

Wrong   Right

Very seldom does a woman say to me that she has "no hips," but if that's your problem, wear skirts with graceful fullness, or pants which fit sleekly without any excess fabric. You may need to find someone skilled at alterations in order to avoid that unattractive gathering of extra fabric between the legs, a danger if your figure isn't full enough to take up the slack. If you have thin hips and no rear end, wear things to soften the line of the hips—like a loose overshirt or open shirt jacket. Skirts are more flattering than pants. Avoid hard-finish fabrics and too strict a look. The mohair and rabbit-hair blends, the velvets, the textured tweeds are for you.

The Bottom

There seem to be limitless ways to emphasize, disguise, decorate or embellish that most expressive of anatomical features—the bottom. One friend, a professional photographer, claims to have made a definitive study of the hundreds of sizes and shapes of perambulating bottoms he has encountered in his travels. He's convinced that he can learn more from watching people from behind than from meeting them head-on. Many people don't have a clear image of how they look from the rear—and some don't *want* to know. Others, who know all too well how they look, take great pains to keep you from seeing. One friend of mine always insists I precede her up a flight of stairs (so I won't be aware of her least favorite feature).

If you have a flat rear end—and this may sound crazy—try wearing trousers backwards, so that the zipper is on the right. Several of my clients find that this works for them. One client told me she couldn't wear knits because, "Look at me! I've got no backside at all!" But when I showed her the look of a bloused two-piece knit with the top overlapping the skirt—a quite different effect from the flat smoothness of the one-piece knit—she was convinced.

Flat Rear End

Wrong   Right

Believe it or not, a pants outfit can even be an advantage in camouflaging a rear end or large hips. It's easier to wear a loose third layer over pants than over a skirt, because length and proportion of the skirt have to be just right for the look to be carried off well. Pants have become a part of our life-style, and I see no reason why vast numbers of women should be hesitant about wearing them. It's a matter of doing it with finesse.

Legs   If you have bow legs, wear skirts a little longer. A soft, fuller skirt or an A-shape is better than a straight line, which would emphasize how *un*straight your legs are. Short legs are best set off in a higher-waisted style. Most of your skirts will need to be taken up. Take care in proportioning your skirt length, because, as we've said before, either too short or too long a skirt tends to further shorten you. You'll want your slacks to be just as long as possible.

We've just talked about a number of ways to minimize figure faults. However, let me stress that there are two ways to deal with them. One is to disguise them, and one is to interpret them. Just as a photographer interprets the truth in reality, so it is important to use illusion in diffusing—or defusing—specific figure problems. Be careful that your clothing does not become a series of masks for various parts of your body.

Sometimes I see a woman who has so thoroughly mastered the methods of camouflaging her body's problems that she's totally dull. She's the one that you *always* see in a navy gabardine pants suit with too long a jacket. Her figure solution is so successful that nobody looks at her. They might not know she has big hips, but who cares? They don't know that she has a personality either—for that, too, is hidden.

Let Clothing Help   Now that you've looked at your body closely, you may feel more
Your Diet Along   aware of its flaws than ever before, and you may be thinking you should do something about it.

Every woman can't have a fantastic body, but every woman can have a better body. The market abounds with books on exercise and diet, and these days there seems to be a health spa on every corner. If you decide you do want to change your body shape, you can even use clothing to inspire you. When some fashion models are trying to lose weight, they deliberately wear clothes that show their extra pounds. That way, even in the kitchen preparing a five-course, gourmet meal, the awareness of their poundage will help to keep them from testing and tasting too much.

Jeans have spelled the downfall of a number of women. Their tight, swaddling effect gives a false sense of security about the body, making you feel athletic and fit even when you're not. Don't be lulled by that feeling and put away another hamburger; if you're wearing jeans, check how you look from all angles in a full-length mirror! For some reason, women seem to be especially blind to the way they look in jeans. Sometimes I don't even notice a client's problem thighs—until I see her in her Levi's!

If you're on a diet, and losing weight around your waist, it's okay to dress "as if" your waist were already a good feature. By dressing that way, you may encourage yourself to make it happen. Of course, don't be overly optimistic—wishing won't do it alone.

The Self-Fulfilling Prophecy

Conversely, by dressing as if your waist were your worst feature, you can help make *that* happen, too. By dressing to conceal a figure flaw, there's always the danger we may let that flaw become worse! I've seen friends who were pregnant hold themselves erect until the day they put on maternity clothes, and then suddenly they felt they had to display a large belly. Their bellies enlarged instantly!

Following the latest behavior techniques in psychology, people all over the country are achieving wonderful results from behaving "as if" they were already more efficient, or happier or loved. This technique can also, within reason, be applied to clothing.

PART III
You And The Language

7
Planning Your Wardrobe

Before we look at the clothes you already have, or even begin to think about shopping for new items, let's discuss a basic wardrobe plan.

It's easy enough just to buy clothes, one outfit at a time, and accumulate lots of things. But do they suit one another? Does that jacket work well with those separate skirts? Do your tops look good with more than just one skirt or one pair of pants? Are the colors coordinated well enough so that you can combine last season's outfits with this season's? Do the accessories add to, and finish, the look?

Does That Outfit Do What It Should?

Can you see an identity in your clothing? Do the pieces and parts reflect who you are? And, on a practical level, do they work for the life you lead? If you're a businesswoman, do you have the right clothes for your normal working schedule? Are they varied enough to avoid boredom and practical enough so you don't have to worry about them at work?

What about your social life? Do you have the right outfits for your favorite activities—sports, concerts or just quiet dinners at the local bistro? Do you have enough casual things so you can dress comfortably but still feel good about the way you look around the house on the weekend?

99

In short, does your wardrobe do what you want it to do?

You may have to spend some money to acquire a basic wardrobe, but once you have it, it will cost you less to maintain than you'd spend buying lots of unrelated pieces, each for its own special use. Although there may still be an occasional event that requires a special purchase, a good basic wardrobe should be able to meet at least ninety-five percent of your clothing needs.

Prerequisites   Each outfit should reflect your own special look, and each should be reliable and reasonably carefree. You want clothes that you can put on in the morning to go to work or to follow your usual routine, clothes that will make you feel good and look good.

A good versatile outfit can be dressed up with the simplest of changes—substituting a silk blouse for a wool one, adding gold or pearl earrings or perhaps a jeweled stickpin at the edge of a lapel.

A matching, pretty blouse and skirt can have the importance of a dress, but with more versatility. Own a sweater and pants in the same classic neutral color as the blouse and skirt (and that can be an interesting color like plum, cinnamon, griege or pale moss), and then you'll have four matching pieces that go with each other easily to make many different combinations. An interesting textured tweed jacket goes over all four. Do you see how a good wardrobe starts to build?

The silk blouse is vital to a functioning wardrobe. You can wear a loose silk shirt as a jacket over another silk shirt and create the very dramatic look of the soft suit, or soft p.j.'s if you're wearing pants. You can get beautiful color combinations this way (like a bright turquoise over a pale red), because silk blouses are available in so many glorious colors. Nowadays, some polyesters can pass for silk, and that can help a limited budget.

Every woman needs a short dress that she feels good in, for all those not too dressy occasions when she used to say, "I don't have the right thing to wear." Years ago it had to be that basic black. Now it can be a soft, ruffled top and gracefully moving skirt in a color that makes you feel feminine and special. Don't choose a color so loud or a print so bold that the outfit becomes too memorable to be worn often. Keep the color and style discreet, and people will compliment you over and over on it, never realizing they've seen it before. A simple outfit lends itself to more creative accessorizing.

A good versatile outfit can be dressed up with the simplest of changes

When I am not going to have time to change before going out in the evening, I take one layer off, or I bring something to work to put over what I have on. My crocheted vest or a shiny belt or earrings for evening work well. Often a higher-heeled, sexier sandal does it. A different cologne also helps to set the evening's mood—you have to work on a mental change as well!

Probably the most versatile garment in my wardrobe is a pair of black-crepe evening pants that I wear with a variety of flattering tops. With a small collection of "look-changers," I am set for many evenings. To vary your outfit, try colored silk cords for a belt, a silk flower, hair clips, different earrings, a few hanging, colored beads and chains worn together.

Although some fashion advisers recommend a lot of identical multiples for your wardrobe, I disagree. You can achieve a kind of uniform for your style that way, and it makes shopping—and getting dressed—easier, but it makes you too predictable. Try to have more than one look in your wardrobe if you are comfortable with the variety. At least let it be a variation upon a theme. Have fun with change and look like fun to others.

Separates

Much versatility and artistry can be achieved by dressing in separates. Separates make a lot of financial sense, too, particularly if you're on a limited budget. Putting all the parts together requires more thought and more planning, but one can build a wardrobe of separates that flows smoothly from day to evening and from one season to the next, even from year to year.

If You Don't Have a Great Deal of Money

If you don't have a great deal of money, it's going to take a bit more time and ingenuity to pull your separates look together. It takes longer to find the one sweater that will go with three different skirts and two pairs of pants, instead of just matching one skirt or one pair of pants. My clients often report with surprise that the sweater we bought for a past season's skirts somehow seems to go with many other pants and skirts bought later on. That's because a consistency of taste and image has been developed, so that separates that were bought at different times suddenly begin to work with one another. It's worth the effort.

In the beginning, however, if your budget's tight, you'll have to think every match through very carefully, rather than have the luxury of its just happening.

A basic tenet in my teaching is to mix one expensive, quality item with some things of lesser quality.

Mixing Quality

Some people who follow this strategy believe that either the shoes or the bag should be the outstanding, costly item. I think it's most important to put the showpiece on top. Wear the expensive item near your face. You can usually get away with an inexpensive skirt, if it fits well, because people don't study it when you're seated or moving. But superior fabric or tailoring in a blouse or jacket will instantly, and consistently, enhance the impression you make.

If you're going out on a date with that new or special man, it's always a good bet to choose a quality blouse or jacket with fine detail on the collars and cuffs. Men seem especially impressed with good tailoring. They also respond immediately to pleasant, bright colors and to soft fabrics.

The most carefully chosen clothing won't do a thing to make you feel or look good unless it fits properly. We've talked about some styling and proportion tricks to help disguise your body flaws. Here are some things to remember about the fit of clothing you'll be wearing.

Getting the Right Fit

Buy clothes that are a little loose, rather than a little tight. Too tight an outfit makes you look uncomfortable and heavier. An exception is a jacket that you never intend to wear closed. That can fit more tightly and help make you look trimmer.

When the look of a garment is deliberately loose, resist the temptation to purchase a much smaller size than you normally wear, just because you're able to fit into it. You'll defeat the whole idea. One size smaller is okay, however, if the look is just too extreme.

A jacket that is perfectly tailored will still look baggy if the sleeves are even a half-inch too long, so check the sleeve length carefully in a full-length mirror. A jacket or coat sleeve should be just long enough to cover the top of the wristbone, letting your blouse cuff peek out a quarter of an inch.

When measuring the length of a skirt hem, don't worry about how many inches it is from the floor, but notice where it hits you on your

Hem Lengths

legs. The shorter your legs, the shorter you can wear your skirts and still stay in overall proportion, though you must always cover the kneecap (until minis come back!).

Color and fabric weight affect the hem length, too. The darker the color or the heavier the fabric, the shorter you should wear it. I don't mean shorter by several inches, but by just a fraction or so, to compensate for the heaviness of the fabric or color. A dark, heavy, melton skirt, for instance, will pull your look down even if it is only half an inch too long. With a lightweight fabric such as silk or cotton gauze, hems can be worn a bit longer. The fabric gives the skirt a floaty look, and you need the extra length so it won't appear too short.

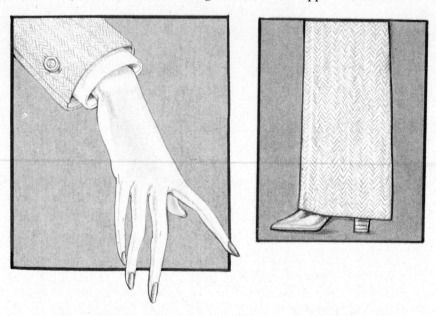

The color of your stockings and shoes will affect the look of a hemline as well as your overall appearance, so be sure to wear the ones you'll be using with the outfit when you decide on the length of the hemline.

For pants, the front hem should touch the top of your shoe, covering the entire instep. The back pant hem can be a little longer, maybe a quarter of an inch. There is nothing that kills the look of any pant outfit, no matter how elegantly put together, more than a pantleg that is too short. If your pants are just a shade too short, it will help to match your stocking color and shoe color to the color of the pants. But if your pants are more than a half-inch too short, nothing will do any good. Fortunately or unfortunately, with today's fashion freedom we have a choice of many different shoes, from flats to high heels, so you'll just have to make a reasonable compromise on the right hem length. If you wear a lot of pants, you could try a reminder note pinned to your pants, stating "with low to medium heels," or "high heels only."

On some of us, the fabric in pants may tend to gap at the small of the back, where the spine curves inward. Lowering the waistband in back by half an inch should make the excess fabric disappear.

One way to vary your basic wardrobe is by adding the right *Accessories* accessories. They can make the same outfit look and feel different, but they, too, must echo your own style. One woman puts on a pair of basic gold loop earrings and a couple of simple gold chains, and she looks overdone, while another woman seems to need some glitter, for she looks just too plain and unpulled together without it.

More at the waist means less at the neck

Never be the lady buried in all the latest clothes or strangled in an excess of jewelry. Sitting across from me the other day in a restaurant was a woman proudly wearing her collection of seven separate jade butterflies of varying sizes. They were perched all over her left shoulder in a mouth-gaping example of over-accessorizing.

The secret is proportion, to your body and to your outfit, and also of one accessory to another. More at the waist, for instance, means less at the neck. More at the neck means less at the waist. All accessories should have a harmony of mood, size, shape, texture and color. They should not only go with each other, but with what you're wearing. The right touch, contrasting or coordinating, or the right color, can make an outfit look really special. Balance touches of glittering gold or iridescent pearls, and add touches of color in a shawl, scarf or sweater vest.

When you put on an outfit, think about whether an accessory change might alter it to advantage. But don't belabor the accessory thing, and don't overplay your theme. For instance, if you start with burgundy accessories, you don't have to hunt up all the other burgundy items you own. Keep your eye on the total look. An old standby rule is, after you're beautifully dressed and accessorized, just before you go out the door, take one thing off!

Scarves   An inexpensive scarf can change your look in a flash. Knotted at the neck, draped over a coat, twisted around the head, tied at the waist, wrapped at the hips—scarves are interesting and they're fun.

But they take practice. Some women are wizards with them. Their scarves seem to stay perfectly in place, casually and creatively knotted and accenting a costume with élan. Other unfortunates, no matter how they try, seem to achieve the effect of a wrinkled, knotted string. Or they look as though they're wearing a bandage around their neck.

If you're not sure about scarves and want to wear them, ease into them slowly. If you're wearing something very plain, like a T-shirt and a cotton print skirt, you could add, at the neck, a little cotton scarf in one of the colors in the skirt to pull the outfit together. If that feels good, experiment with other scarves in other colors and sizes with other outfits.

Don't loop a scarf just once. Only a square knot will keep it steady. (Tie its ends left over right and right over left.) To stop a scarf from

slipping, anchor it secretly with tiny safety pins and it won't move around on you.

You can tie the square knot close to your neck and centered in the front, or you can push the knot jauntily to the side and have the accent of the two little ties coming out of the collar. The triangle in the back of the scarf should be tucked inside the collar. If you have a larger square scarf, you can wear it loose, in a middy effect by tying the square knot lower down on your chest.

A wool scarf hanging loosely over a raincoat may be very effective. Don't always tuck your scarves neatly into your coats like an ascot. It's too stiff and uptight looking.

You can wear scarves in your hair folded on the bias and wrapped around the head like a turban. Tie a scarf around the hair like a ribbon, or twist it and use it like a headband.

Never, never wear chiffon scarves, unless they are the kind that trail down the back of some luxurious evening gown. Otherwise they are

always tacky and look as though they should be worn over curlers. The only use for a chiffon scarf is to protect your makeup and hair as you pull clothing over your head (as I explain later in the shopping chapter).

On some women, a hat bestows dignity, charm and distinction, and it makes their eyes more important. But other women lose their carefree femininity when their hair is all covered up and restricted by a hat.

People either are comfortable in hats or they're not. If you are, wear hats and enjoy them. Hats provide a good way to create an instant image. Put one on, you've got a totally new look; take it off, you've changed again! It's a nice way to transform your appearance from day to evening.

The right hat seems to look better and better as it becomes more and more you. However, be sure *you* don't become more and more the *hat,* for hats have a way of taking over. At least two people I know seem to have theirs glued permanently on top. This is emotional dependence, not style.

Personally, I do not wear hats, for a very definite reason. Hats tend to make quite a strong fashion statement; I don't enjoy looking so typecast that the moment I walk into a room I'm classified as someone who is in fashion.

Do wear belts, both wide and narrow, if your figure allows. Remember, a heavy midriff can be belted if you're wearing a loose third layer. Tawny calfskin, glittering chains, silky ribbon sashes—they can really finish an outfit or even be the focal point of that outfit.

A good belt wardrobe that should carry you through the four seasons and give you enough variety would include:

1. The most important—about a ¾" width, luggage-color leather, classic belt with a simple, gold buckle. (Buy it a bit wider if you have a midriff roll.) If you can afford only one belt, this is it.
2. A soft-suede, wrap, contour belt, in burgundy or mahogany, perhaps.
3. A gold-combined-with-silver, all-in-one, narrow metallic belt.
4. A black, evening rope belt.

In summer, add one narrow white belt, perhaps one narrow red belt for some accenting fun, and a great all-purpose straw rope-belt.

The little belt can act as a third layer, which so many of my clients rightfully admit really helps them finish an outfit. It can transform a

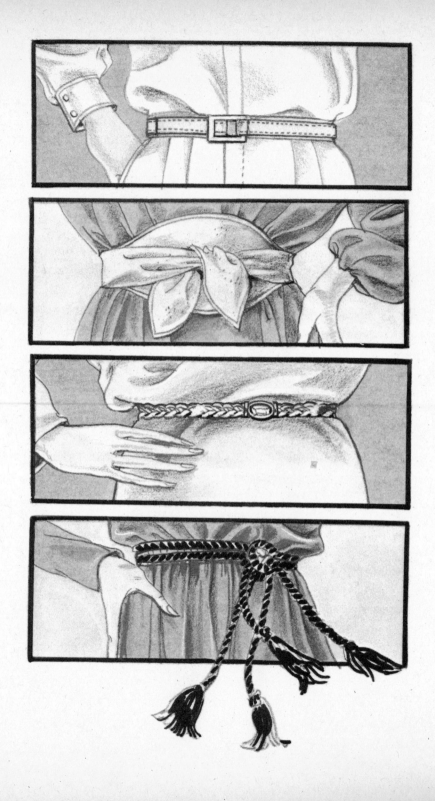

blouse and skirt into a flattering ensemble. That same belt would also be the only accessory needed with the skirt you wear with a simple sweater. The accent of a belt sometimes performs a minor miracle.

You'll note that this suggested shoe wardrobe contains several open-toed shoes. They are flattering, and are okay to wear year-round now—indoors. Wear boots to get where you're going. You can keep open-toed shoes at work and change into them.

1. Luggage-leather walking shoes for sporty skirts and pants. (Perhaps with slightly tweedy, textured hose that blends into the shoe color.)
2. Luggage spectator pumps.
3. Black-lizard-texture (for shine interest), closed-toed slingbacks.
4. Burgundy/mahogany, open-toed, day-to-evening sandal. For summer, substitute a white, open-toed, slingback sandal and a red, strippy, medium-high sandal.
5. One pair rubber rainboots (in shiny black, or even a bright shiny red).
6. One pair of winter leather boots, medium-high heel, in black or luggage, depending on your coat color.

1. Medium-large, luggage-leather shoulder bag (for day).
2. Luggage-leather, medium-size clutch.
3. Burgundy, medium-size pouch clutch.
4. Black-fabric evening clutch.

Basically, shoes and bags should match and should be bought in a classic, all-purpose color. Luggage or mahogany are more interesting, I think, than just dull, dark brown. Shiny black, burgundy and taupe are all-purpose, too, and red and creamy white for summer.

A match between shoes and bags need not be a perfect one, but the color family should be the same. The eye will tend to complete the optical illusion of the nearly matching colors because it wants the two items to go together.

In spring and summer, you can wear a textured bag, such as straw, with any color shoes. Straw is always relatively inexpensive, and some straw clutch bags can be worn with evening wear as easily as with sports clothes. The natural texture goes with every spring and summer color. So if you're carrying a straw bag and wearing luggage-leather sandals, they're not going to match, but that's all right. It would be

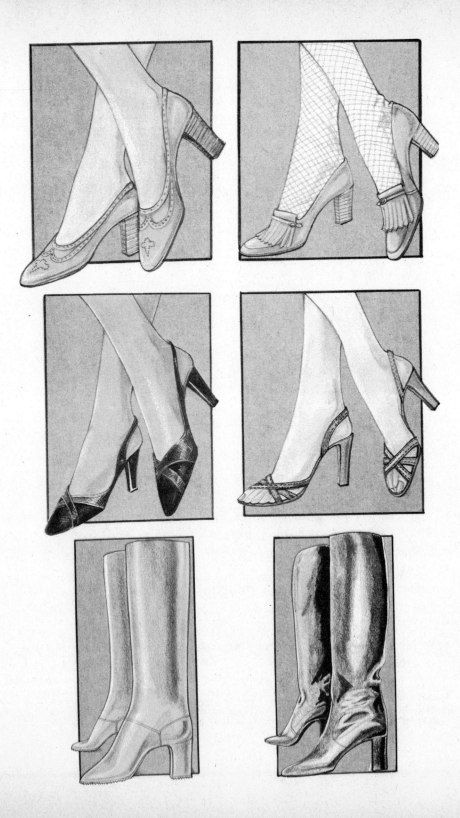

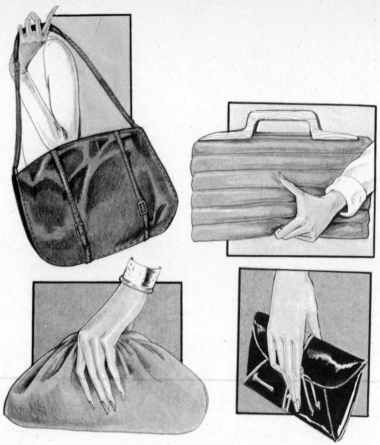

great if you could find a luggage-trimmed straw bag and then match it to luggage sandals, but that's tough to do.

It's okay to pair a patent-leather bag and leather shoes, or vice versa. So long as it's the same color, it doesn't have to be patent with patent. Leather with suede is also fine, if they are in the same color family.

Stockings   The best all-around color for stockings is one that is a shade darker than your natural skin color. The stocking texture should go with the mood of your shoe—a rough-textured country stocking with a low-heel walking loafer and a sheerer stocking as your heel gets higher and the shoe becomes more delicate.

Jewelry   Never underestimate the importance of jewelry. One day I was trying several looks on a client, and nothing seemed to click. Then I

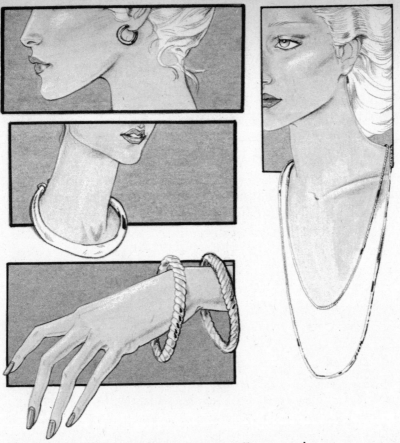

tried a pair of simple, gold-loop earrings. She seemed to grow up and become important looking with just that small addition.

Your only essentials are a set of those earrings, two gold chains, a gold tubular choker, and a bangle or two. I happen to think that, on most women, gold makes a more important statement than silver. You can also use jewelry in one or two colors. I have one set of jewelry accessories in jade—a pendant, beads and earrings—and another set in garnet with gold—a stickpin, earrings, bracelet and a ring. I wear them whenever I need a touch of color.

Clients frequently ask me what they should do with a diamond engagement ring, or a diamond brooch that their husbands gave them. I feel diamonds often look out of place with the informality of our present life-style and dress. Sometimes I see a woman wearing a huge diamond with a housedress. The dress may be completely inappropriate, but she tells herself, "I still look okay, even though I'm wearing this shoddy outfit, because I'm sporting my 3-carat diamond ring."

Diamonds are beautiful, and diamonds are forever, but I think it's best, on some informal occasions, to leave them at home.

One Item Can Make the Outfit

I have a friend who borrowed an expensive, silver Moroccan belt whenever she wanted to look special. Even though she was on a limited budget, it eventually became clear to her that it made a lot of sense to invest in such a belt herself. If a hundred-dollar belt can make you feel like a million, it's a bargain! It can take the anxiety out of getting ready for those special occasions.

You can further express your creativity and your style by wearing your own hand-crafted clothing or jewelry. Wear it, however, only if it really speaks you. You may be skilled at a craft that looks better on someone else. And never wear too much of it at one time or you'll cancel out its effect. The woman who is hand-crocheted from head to foot looks really homemade.

Other Vital Accessories

Hair, makeup and hands are also accessories to your clothing, whether you want them to be or not. Hair is a particularly prominent and powerful accessory. How often one is labeled by hair color alone—"that well-dressed blonde," "that cute redhead." And you know how awful you feel when your hair looks bad. If you can wear a number of different hair styles, take the extra effort to change your hair occasionally, if only for the creative exercise involved.

Coordinate your makeup with your ensemble. Lipstick and eye shadow bring the color from your outfit up to your face in the best possible way and can certainly accentuate your own eye color. Make sure your lipstick isn't of a color that contrasts in too glaring a way with the clothes color you're wearing. Bright lipsticks are nice, but not if they dominate your whole appearance. And if you are wearing a bright shade, for goodness sake make sure you draw a well-defined lip line. If your lips are large, lipstick should be less bright.

If your hands are good, indulge in rings, nail polish, interesting bracelets or ruffled cuffs that draw the eye. If you have hands you don't want to draw attention to, then forget fashion and avoid the jewelry.

Your scent might be called a highly evocative accessory. I don't believe one should change scents as often as you change an outfit. It's really a rather personalized signature. Choosing one's own scent seems to be a way of establishing individuality (a woman seldom wears a scent that her mother wore). Sometimes, though, I think it's a nice idea to change to a new perfume when a chapter in your life has ended and you're ready to begin a new one.

Basic
Winter and Summer
Wardrobes

When I began my business eight years ago, I used to tell my clients that it would take a minimum of $500 to put together a fall or spring wardrobe. Now, unhappily, I have to advise them that it may take approximately twice that. Although costs change, I am indicating some prices here to show relative quality. You may wish to spend a good deal less or a good deal more.

Here are four basic wardrobes, illustrated to show the relationship of every garment to the others. For the most complicated of the wardrobes (the winter basic wardrobe for a working woman), I will describe the thought process involved. Whatever the individual aspects of your own particular wardrobe, the same principles are involved. If you want to build on burgundy instead of brown tweed and camel, just make the appropriate changes. Remember—these are examples only. You must select your wardrobe based on your individual needs, body type, and—most important—your own style.

Winter Wardrobe of a Working Woman

(The Thought Process)

Jackets

I'm advising two well-tailored jackets, both of which can be worn over work outfits and one of which can go dressy. They will be of different color families and different textures. For my example, I've chosen the simplest basic of a brown tweed jacket and a black-velvet jacket.

Skirts

Skirts are important in the separates wardrobe of a working girl. One might be a classic camel, feminized by a few kicky pleats, the other a rabbit-hair or textured, softly gathered skirt—if you can wear this line. (The point is that the skirts should be of different shapes.) For the third skirt, choose, perhaps, a brown or wine abstract-print, wool challis; or a velvet print which, combined with the black velvet blazer, will make a lovely separates evening outfit. You've now begun to achieve a basic core wardrobe, with a balance of print, color and texture.

Pants   If you can wear pants to work, make sure to achieve a totally finished look that's formal but not necessarily strict. I chose a tweed pant to match the tweed blazer, because I love that look with soft sweaters for weekend life, as well. One good pair of black wool pants is essential if you wear pants at all, for casual evenings as well as for work, with a different texture of black in your velvet blazer.

Blouses   Prepare a few changes in blouses. As important as a tie change is to a man's outfit, blouses are affordable and yet can change a whole look quickly (see illustration page 101). Blouses are the way to introduce a note of beautiful color into your wardrobe language when the length of a dress in the same color would be too overbearing and certainly more costly.

One good, classic item is a pretty cream silk blouse. It can have a small bow or a well-tailored collar—whatever. But you've got to love it, and be able to pull for it often, even for evenings with your black pants and velvet jacket. This blouse can be used as the most useful classic under your third layers, your suede jerkin and your sweater vest.

Another practical blouse on my list is the honey-brown, solid, ruffle-neck blouse; it can fill nearly all the slots that your cream classic fills. The only reason it is second on the list is that it is more memorable since it's a color, and thus can't be worn quite as often. These two blouses should go with all three skirts *and* your two pairs of pants.

Next, buy a blouse in a small print, which should go with both your day skirts and your brown tweed blazer. If you're clever in choosing the print, it should work well under your jerkin and sweater vest as well. I chose a small, classic foulard or a stripe, because these subtle patterns can be worn next to tweed. If the two patterns seem busy at your face, you can help the situation by adding a solid-brown neck scarf or solid-color turtleneck dickey.

Now that you've got your classics and your touch of print, it would be nice to add a splash of color. Cranberry is a good choice to go with the color families of brown and black.

The last blouse to acquire for a complete basic wardrobe would be a solid colored sheer, billowy evening overblouse, perhaps tied with a peplum effect, and with a drawstring neckline that you can sometimes leave open. It should have full, feminine sleeves (they *will* fit under your covering of black-velvet jacket, because they are sheer). This evening blouse can be worn with your good black pants.

Your third layer—your suede jerkin and your softer-textured, rabbit-hair sweater vest are useful to carry a theme, or whenever you don't want to wear a jacket. You can vary the look with a narrow leather belt at the waist over the sweater vest, to make a slightly more formal appearance. Most of us welcome the fact that both of these third layers can be best worn outside the skirts or trousers to camouflage our hips or stomach.

Third Layers

A soft sweater dress, in a color such as mauve or forest green, is a balancing touch of femininity. If your figure isn't too ample in any one place, and if your sweater dress fits loosely enough, I don't see why a cowlneck, soft, classic sweaterdress can't be worn to work. And either color would be good under your tweed blazer.

Dresses

For a second selection, let's get a darkish, small-to-medium print dress. It could have a peasant smocking effect at the neck, but not too full sleeves, and not that midi, ruffle hemline, or you won't be able to wear it to work. A dark, floral-print challis would be a great balance to your tailored wardrobe. And your black velvet jacket is perfect over it.

After dark, you'll need two better dresses that you can feel especially good in—perhaps a two-piece, sheer-wool banana color skirt and its own soft top (I suggest a two-piece because the top can probably be worn as a separate blouse). The blouse could do with some pretty detail on its collar, like a fragile cutout pattern or some embroidery in the same banana color. Banana, or a similar classic shade, will coordinate with both your sporty and your dressy jackets.

A silk dress with a bow or fine tucking will be your print balance for those work-to-evening needs. A small, darker print would, again, be the most practical and flattering in the winter—great under your black velvet. But do sometimes wear these feminine fabric dresses without jackets for a refreshing change, even at work.

Basic Winter Wardrobe for Working Woman

	Column A	Column B	Column C
		Clothes in Column B Go With Clothes in Columns A and/or C	
2 COATS $225	Basic Trench Raincoat $100	Black Coat $125 *Day to evening*	
2 JACKETS $140	Brown Tweed Jacket $80 *Bought with matching pants, as pant-suit*		Black Velvet Jacket $60
4 BLOUSES $175	Brown on Cream Small Geometric Print $25	Cream Classic Blouse $40 Cranberry Bow Blouse $35 Honey Drawstring Neck Blouse $35	Solid Sheer Evening Overblouse $40
2 SWEATERS $50	Camel Cowlneck Sweater $25 Medium-Brown Turtleneck Sweater $25		
2 THIRD LAYERS	Brown Suede Jerkin $35		

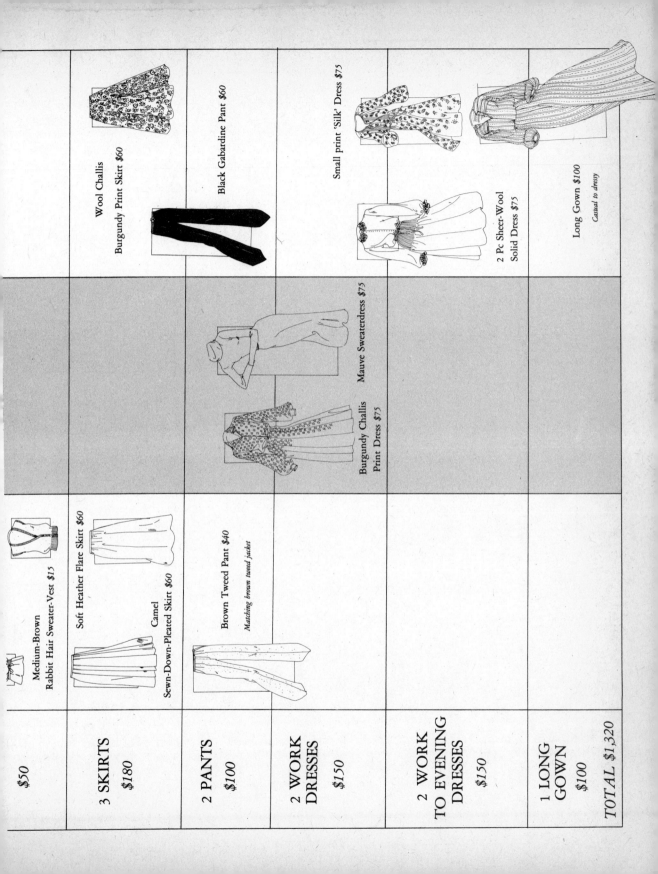

$50

Medium-Brown Rabbit Hair Sweater-Vest $15

3 SKIRTS $180

Soft Heather Flare Skirt $60

Camel Sewn-Down-Pleated Skirt $60

Wool Challis Burgundy Print Skirt $60

2 PANTS $100

Brown Tweed Pant $40

Matching brown tweed jacket

Black Gabardine Pant $60

2 WORK DRESSES $150

Burgundy Challis Print Dress $75

Mauve Sweaterdress $75

2 WORK TO EVENING DRESSES $150

Small print 'Silk' Dress $75

2 Pc Sheer-Wool Solid Dress $75

1 LONG GOWN $100

Long Gown $100

Casual to dressy

TOTAL $1,320

Basic Winter Wardrobe for Non-working Woman

	Column A	Column B Clothes in Column B Go With Clothes in Columns A and or C	Column C
2 COATS $225	Storm Coat $100	Black Coat $125 *Day to evening*	
2 JACKETS $120	Brown Tweed $80 *Bought with matching pant, as a pant-suit*		Cream Sweater Jacket $40
3 BLOUSES $105	Brown on Cream Small Print Bow Blouse $25	Cream Classic Blouse $40	Evening Solid Overblouse $40 *Choose a color to go with brown/black tweed long skirt and black pants*
3 SWEATERS $75	Soft Brown Scoop Neck Sweater $25	Cream Turtleneck $25	Black Cowlneck $25

| 1 SKIRT | Soft Brown Heather Skirt $60 | | |
| $60 | | | |

| 4 PANTS | Brown Tweed Pant $40 *Matching blazer* | Camel Pant $60 | Casual Jean $45 | Black Gabardine Pant $60 |
| $205 | | | | |

| 1 DRESS | | Mauve Sweater Dress $75 |
| $75 | | *Any color that goes with brown tweed jacket and cream sweater jacket* |

| 1 LONG SKIRT | | Brown/Black Tweed Long Skirt $50 |
| $50 | | |

TOTAL $915

Basic Summer Wardrobe for Working Woman

	Column A	Column B	Column C
1 RAINCOAT $100		*Clothes in Column B Go With Clothes in Columns A and/or C* Black Summer Raincoat $100 *Day to evening*	
2 OUTER LAYERS $95		White Jacket $60 *Bought as suit with white skirt to match* Solid Color Shawl $35 *Choose a color to go with 3 blouse prints and the 2 skirt prints*	
6 BLOUSES $165	Plaid Shirt $25 Stripe Shirt $25 Floral Print $25 *Choose prints to go with your solid color skirts, as well as your white skirt and pant*	Solid Blouse $25 Solid Color Blouse $25 Solid Color Blouse $25 *Choose colors to go with your solid color skirt, and your 2 print skirts* Solid Color Sheer Evening Blouse $40	

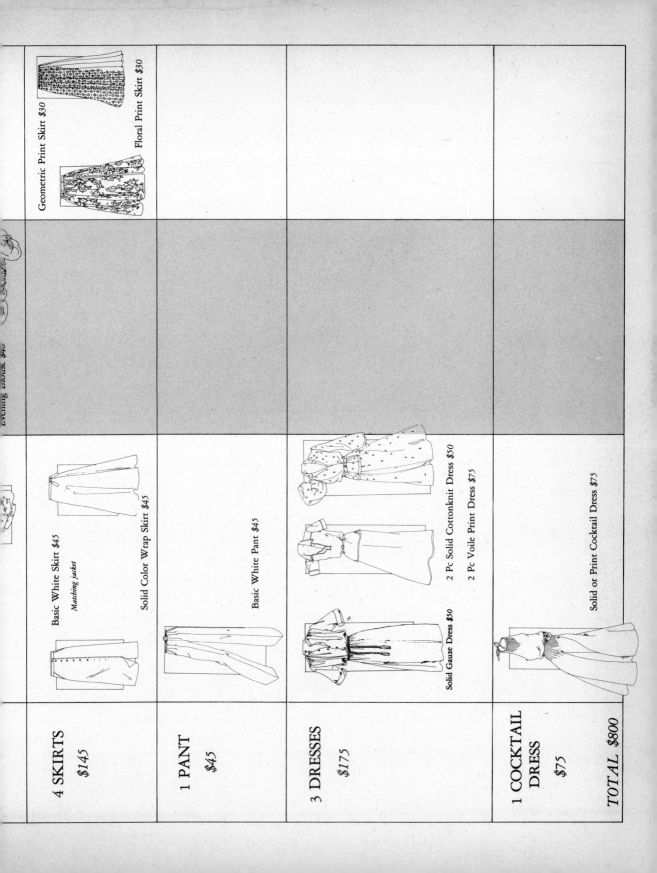

Geometric Print Skirt $30 — Floral Print Skirt $30

Basic White Skirt $45 (Matching jacket) — Solid Color Wrap Skirt $45

Basic White Pant $45

Solid Gauze Dress $50 — 2 Pc Solid Cottonknit Dress $50 — 2 Pc Voile Print Dress $75

Solid or Print Cocktail Dress $75

4 SKIRTS $145

1 PANT $45

3 DRESSES $175

1 COCKTAIL DRESS $75

TOTAL $800

Basic Summer Wardrobe for Non-working Woman

	Column A	Column B	Column C	Column D
1 OUTER LAYER $35		Clothes in Column B Go With Clothes in Columns A and/or C *Day to evening* Solid Color Shawl $35		*Your evening cover-up will be the same solid color shawl*
4 BLOUSES $115	 Plaid Shirt $25 Floral Blouse $25 *Choose colors to go with cinnamon, as well as white pant and skirt*	 Solid Color Blouse $25 *This color should go with the print skirts, cinnamon pant, and of course the white skirt and pant*		*Choose a print that goes with solid color shawl* Evening Print Overblouse $40
3 UNDERTOPS $40		 Solid Camisole $10 Solid T-Shirt $15 Solid T-Shirt $15 		*Choose colors that go with solid color shawl*

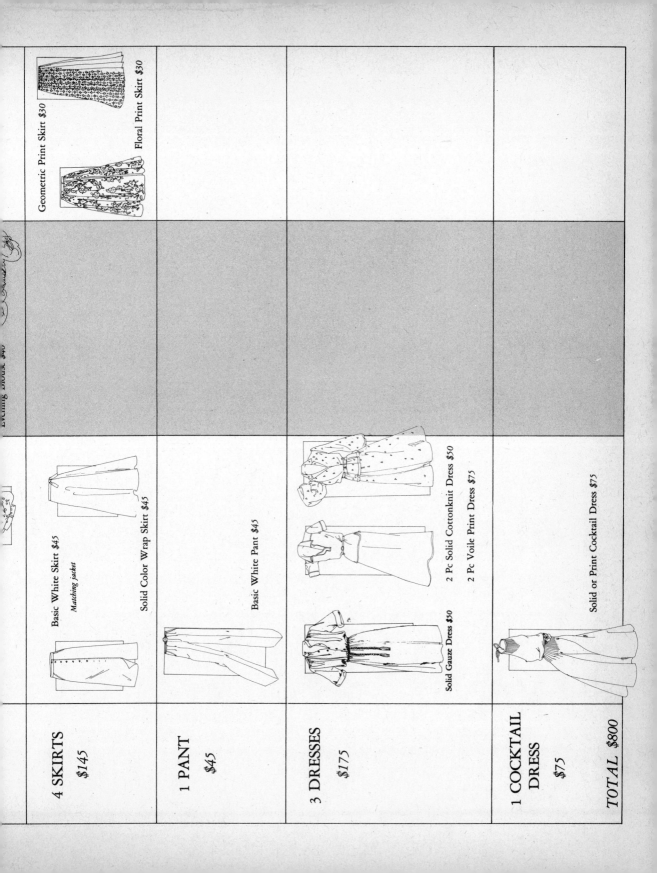

Geometric Print Skirt $30

Floral Print Skirt $30

Evening Blous $40

4 SKIRTS $145

Basic White Skirt $45

Matching jacket

Solid Color Wrap Skirt $45

1 PANT $45

Basic White Pant $45

3 DRESSES $175

Solid Gauze Dress $50

2 Pc Solid Cottonknit Dress $50

2 Pc Voile Print Dress $75

1 COCKTAIL DRESS $75

Solid or Print Cocktail Dress $75

TOTAL $800

Basic Summer Wardrobe for Non-working Woman

	Column A	Column B	Column C	Column D
1 OUTER LAYER $35		Clothes in Column B Go With Clothes in Columns A and/or C *Day to evening* Solid Color Shawl $35		*Your evening cover-up will be the same solid color shawl*
4 BLOUSES $115	Plaid Shirt $25 Floral Blouse $25 *Choose colors to go with cinnamon, as well as white pant and skirt*	Solid Color Blouse $25 *This color should go with the print skirts, cinnamon pant, and of course the white skirt and pant*		*Choose a print that goes with solid color shawl* Evening Print Overblouse $40
3 UNDERTOPS $40		Solid Camisole $10 Solid T-Shirt $15 Solid T-Shirt $15		
			Choose colors that go with solid color shawl	

3 SKIRTS $105		
Basic White Skirt $40	Floral Print Skirt $30 Geometric Print Skirt $30	

3 PANTS $135		Black Evening Pant $45
Basic White Pant $45 Cinnamon Color Pant $45		

1 COCKTAIL DRESS $100		
Not too dressy so it will be more versatile		
Cocktail Dress $100		

TOTAL $530

Your long gown should be functional for events more casual than black-tie dinners, but it should also be able to be dressed up to more glamour with the addition of jewelry or flowers or ribbons. Think about the simplicity of a pale, dust-rose-silk, loose, easy top and long flowing skirt in matching solid silk. Get the thought process?

Coats   Perhaps you can't afford a long coat to wear over your gown this season, but, for now, your velvet jacket will do admirably, maybe with a soft, woolly, shawl over it for warmth. (Let's hope you will just be jumping in and out of a car so you won't freeze.)

Or, alternately, you may find the ideal black, wet-look, flared tent of a simple raincoat, which will not only go over your browns and blacks but is even glamorous enough, because of the shine and the loose, simple cut, to wear over dresses in the evening.

If black flatters you, and you don't have pets that shed, a good black coat is the best choice for outer wear that has to span both day and evening hours. My second recommendation in coat color for this wardrobe is a reddish-mahogany-brown; that color will coordinate with your browns and blacks as well as with wines (if that's one of the colors you're building around—your eye will pick up the red in the mahogany). I like it so much better than a plain dark brown, which you would not be able to wear in combination with black.

Basic accessories for winter, taken from the list already illustrated, and not included in the cost estimate, would be a medium-luggage school clutch with wrist strap, and a soft pouch in suede. A belt would be your classic narrow, luggage belt and your gold-and-silver slink belt. Shoes are a pair of gillies (lady loafers) with wood, medium heel, a spectator, luggage pump, burgundy open-toed sandals, closed-toed, black-lizard slingbacks and one pair of boots.

Now that you know what your ideal future wardrobe should consist of (and the thought process that got you there), you need to determine what usable things you already have, what can be *made* usable and how. You need to take into consideration the requirements of your particular life-style and how all of this fits in with that all-important factor, your budget.

8
Your Closet, Your Budget, Your Life-Style

When the man seated next to me on the plane asked the reason for my trip, I felt a little foolish explaining that I was headed for North Carolina for the day, just to clean out somebody's closet. I'm not sure he believed me. I know he didn't understand how important it was.

I had received a telephone call a few days earlier from a man who wanted to give his wife an extra-special birthday present. She had read about me in *Parade* magazine and had shown him the article. He paid my air fare and the fee, and I flew down to help his wife find her new image.

My new client turned out to be a lavishly clothed woman with a closet the size of my living room. I spent four straight hours in that closet, sorting out dozens of dresses and really grubbing around on the floor, opening boxes and hauling out stored-away garments. Some of them dated back as far as the fifties. They were all of fabulous quality and in perfect condition; they still fit well and had cost so much money that their owner simply couldn't bring herself to get rid of them. But she probably never would be able to wear any of them again—her image had changed too much through the years. I told Mrs. Keaton that, even though she had the space in her closet, it cluttered up her mind to have all those options around that weren't viable.

Closets are marvelous indicators of personality. After I've spent some time in a new client's closet, I probably know more about her than I learn about a social acquaintance in a year's time. If what someone is wearing makes a statement about her, surely her closet is a whole volume! All of a person's habits and tastes, priorities, efficiency, economic sense and aesthetic and material values are laid out on wire, wooden or padded-satin, monogrammed hangers. In my glimpses of some of the finest closets in the East, I've seen sights ranging from sixty pairs of shoes lined up in neat rows to tangled masses of mink, and chiffon gowns, thrown in a jumbled heap on the floor.

Evaluation of a client's present wardrobe is the first step of my service. As in any profession that offers a service, there's often an initial distrust on the part of the client. Another woman is coming into her home to look into her closet, poke through her jewelry box, ask her personal questions about why she's not pleased about her image, and then make suggestions about how she should dress! I suspect almost anyone would be uncomfortable.

As quickly as possible, I try to let my anxious client know that my aim is not to criticize her but to help. And her trust often comes with hearing just one on-the-mark statement. Each woman hears truth in a different way.

The Closet Orgy   All right now, let's look at *your* closet. Everything out—everything out of the plastic bags and the boxes on the shelves and the dresser drawers. It's an orgy of try-ons! Let's find out what does and what doesn't fit your body or your personality. If it isn't right, let's get rid of it. Allow yourself at least an hour or two for this activity, and try to think of it as a pleasant task. It should be a good feeling to clarify one's life.

Do try on even your favorite clothes. Perhaps you're sure that they're okay, but slip them on anyhow. If they do feel right—and fit well—if they look good, and express the aspects of your personality you want to show, then you know what the right clothing for you feels like. Remember that feeling. Remember the pleasure that comes with wearing something wonderful, and resolve that never again will you buy anything that doesn't give you that special feeling. There's no reason to compromise.

It's generally a good idea to start by trying on your suits, or at least the more costly garments that you're planning to build your wardrobe around. Be sure to try the suit jackets with different skirts and pants, and vice versa, checking out all possible combinations.

Then consider what you need to buy in order to make fuller use of these favorite garments. If you don't have enough blouses to build around that good standby suit, then you're really not taking advantage of the money that you spent for it. A sheer floral print, for instance, might let that suit go right from day into evening, and double its use and value to you.

Some people need to do a good deal of weeding out. One client kept *Weeding Out* a shirt that she claimed to have had from the age of twelve! The sleeves came up to her elbows and it barely buttoned across her chest, but she was delighted to think she could still "fit" into it. I put that into the category of nostalgia. Momentos are fine, but they ought to be labeled as such and kept out of the closet.

I thought I was so smart when I bought my short, lace wedding dress. Out of a naive sense of practicality, I compromised my years of dreaming about gliding down the aisle in a long wedding gown. I had the romantic notion I would wear my short wedding dress for every anniversary dinner. But in one year the lace dress that I loved was too short and the scoop neck was no longer me. Both the fashion and the bride had changed a lot in that one year.

We know that life means change, and yet possessions from bygone *Life Means Change* days are found in almost every home, stuffed into closets or under beds, and crammed into dresser drawers. Why? It's one thing to keep old favorites stored away in the basement or attic, if you're lucky enough to have one. But if you insist on keeping them right alongside the garments you consider day-to-day, as if it were still possible to wear them, you're putting your yesterdays ahead of today. Old, broken bits of well-loved jewelry fall into this category, too. Broken necklaces and odd earrings don't take up much space, but they keep you from getting a clear look at the jewelry you do have. I think it's important to lighten up and let go. And when we do get rid of these old things, it gives us such an exhilarating feeling.

Mistakes   There are some things in your closet that need to be discarded not because they're old, but because they're plain and simple mistakes. Something that may have looked wonderful in the store, under a spotlight, on the latest mod manikin may not have looked quite the same when you got it home.

Remember that mistakes do not correct themselves simply because you do penance. Opening your closet each morning and being confronted with masses of mistakes is not good for the soul, and it certainly is no way to make dressing a pleasant activity.

Filene's in Boston, which is world-famous for its bargain basement, has a system of time-tagging clothes, reducing the price of an item every few days it stays there and finally just about giving it away. You might think about that sort of system yourself—moving little-used clothing to the back of the closet. Then, if it hasn't been worn in a given length of time, get rid of it. I've found it's almost a sure bet that if you haven't worn something in two years, you're not going to. That item should relinquish its space to something new in your life.

Don't Hang Your Albatross Around Someone Else's Neck   Sometimes it helps to give the item to a daughter or to a friend. Just be sure you're not hanging your albatrosses around somebody else's neck. It may be better to donate impersonally to a local charity which will give you a written estimate of the value of the gift, so that you can write it off on your income tax. In any event, don't hang onto that beloved old coat or dress until you're able to find just the perfect recipient—it might take years!

Clothing Has a Personality All Its Own   Some clothing seems to have a personality all its own. One dress is quite benign, friendly and dependable, waiting patiently in the closet for you to make use of it. Another outfit seems to be hostile, attracts spots like a magnet, deliberately opens its seams (usually in a sneaky way under the arms), develops creases across the lap and even insists upon falling off its hanger. It clenches its zippered teeth in a rage so you can't even get out of the bloody thing, and it's the first to announce with glee that you've just gained two pounds.

Well, don't put up with it. Any piece of clothing that ungrateful should be tossed out unceremoniously. No matter what it cost, or whether others think it's attractive, you know its true nature. If you're miserable in it, get rid of it.

If a dress looks like dynamite on you but is uncomfortable after a while, make a point of wearing it around the house for a couple of hours, perhaps at a dinner at home. Then take a good look at yourself in a mirror. If there's a frown on your face, or a sore, red spot on the back of your neck from its scratchy fabric, the glamour isn't worth it.

Don't get hung up by that god, quality. Admit you made a mistake when you bought that black faille dress. If the truth were known, you thought it was a little dreary even then, but you wanted to be known as someone with quiet good taste. That dress is so subdued, however, it's been putting people to sleep. If a garment is wrong for you, not fabric or workmanship or designer labels or a chain of diamonds is going to make it right. Move on. Quality alone doesn't make it.

Quality Alone Doesn't Make It

Then there are some passé dresses, constructed so heavily that they don't even seem to need you. Some of them could stand by themselves right in the middle of the room, *sans* body, and look just fine. If it's a dress that doesn't need *you,* then *you* don't need *it.*

Sometimes a garment is okay in every respect, except that it duplicates something else in your wardrobe. If you have several items that fulfill the same purpose for the same kind of occasion, and state more or less the same message, there will almost invariably be one favorite, and you'll find that you keep putting that one on and letting the others sit there.

Duplicates

Think about passing some of these extras along to somebody else who could use them—for you probably won't.

Some women seem to slide up and down the scale constantly. This season they may be size 10, but two years ago it was 12, or 14. They may own as many as three complete wardrobes, each in a different size. Women in this situation have often asked me if they should keep all those "extras" on hand.

The Vital Question of Weight

If weight gain is a fear, my advice is to keep the smaller size in the closet, and store the larger ones. You might make the grand gesture of tossing out your "fat" clothes, but who can afford to do it over and over again? It is also psychologically risky to keep those big clothes too available; I'd put them somewhere harder to get at than in your closet.

If you're currently at the weighty end of the scale and wearing the larger wardrobe, keep favorites from that skinny set of clothes right in the closet where you see them every day. It should help as a reminder of what you want to achieve.

Alterations Generally, size alterations are the only ones that actually work. Altering a style is risky, and it rarely succeeds. Unless you really have the eye, don't try it. Sometimes a favorite coat can be cut successfully to jacket length, but if there's something basically wrong with the garment, forget it.

You may be able to get more wear out of a long velvet or wool skirt by cutting it to midi length to wear with boots for the fall and winter. When the skirt shape is too full, or a dress is too long-waisted, an alteration is feasible. If a dress starts to wrinkle below the waist, you may think the dress should be made tighter. This only makes the wrinkling worse. Instead, the waistline should be picked up, for the dress is slightly long-waisted on you.

As a rule, an alteration is not feasible when the collar is too large and the wrong shape, if the pants are too short in the crotch, or if a jacket is too short-waisted. Usually, dresses that are too short-waisted can't be fixed unless there's a generous seam allowance. Any alteration that attempts to change the essential line of the garment is a useless undertaking.

Many synthetic knits and plush fabrics like velvet can't be let out because stitch impressions of the original seams show.

Adding a border to a skirt works only occasionally. If you're fortunate enough to have extra fabric, the piece can be added and the only problem is that the old, short hemline shows. A clever solution to hide the line of a let-down hem is to add a topstitched seam-detail addition. That always works out well, and can lend an expensive-looking touch to the garment. However, most of the time we don't have the extra matching fabric, and adding a contrast of any kind, no matter how close a match, looks like the patch job it is.

For any large alteration job, I believe that real expertise is necessary. Either we have it in the sewing department or we don't. My own sewing is a bit like the story that author Jane Siddons tells: "In shortening a cocktail dress recently," she says, "I painstakingly sewed the front to the silk lining in the back, producing inside the dress proper a sort of glorified silk potato sack."

One pitfall facing the amateur seamstress is taking on too much, believing she can fix almost any fault in a garment. As a shopper, she often takes a technical approach, checking only on how well something is made, instead of standing back and looking at the total impression that garment makes.

The Ghost of That Dress May Follow You

If there's a dress that you've held onto for years with the thought that it just needs a little fixing, that it's still in "good shape" and could be used somehow—perhaps as a cut off blouse or a skirt—you probably just plain don't like it. And when you've hated something for years, its ghost is going to follow you, no matter how much you've done to make it different. So out it goes.

Updating Older Clothing

As we're closet cleaning, you'll probably come across older clothing that just needs a little pizzazz. Try adding accessories. Add a belt or scarf to an old cardigan sweater, and you might affect the look of a chic 1930s sweater jacket. Don't try things like putting an old mini dress over a pair of slacks to simulate a tunic—that doesn't fool anyone.

Do try punctuating with some ingenuity, like a new color combination, a flower, or a happy print. Use small neck scarves or sweaters to wear inside some of your shirts to change their look. And why shouldn't a heavier fabric blouse act as a shirt jacket when worn over a lighter one? If the heavier shirt has a straight, finished bottom, then it can be left open or buttoned partway from the bottom and belted on the outside. If the bottom shouldn't be seen, fold it under all the way around and tie the shirt ends in front in a square knot.

Add a belt to an old cardigan sweater

We have said before that you might use a solid-color turtleneck dickey or neck scarf to make a print blouse less busy, or coordinate a print shirt and a solid-color skirt. Sometimes a commonplace peasant work smock, worn in a different setting, becomes a treasure. I have an inexpensive, delicate, hand-crocheted vest from Hong Kong that makes many of my outfits special.

One shirt over another

Roll up the sleeves of an old shirt if they're frayed or short; it's a nice nonchalant look. Or use a favorite old shirt for its collar only, inside a scoop-necked pullover, for a touch of its print or color near your face.

If you cut down a full long skirt to midi length, make the cut-off part (if it's large enough) into an oblong shawl. Add a touch of fringe at both ends, and you'll have a very nice ensemble.

When pants are too short and you're going to feel all day that people are looking at your "high-waters," it's better to tuck them into a pair of boots for the knickers look.

Old panty hose with runs can be cut off and worn under slacks, or under skirts of thin, clingy fabrics to make a truly seamless underpant. (I learned that trick years ago from another photography stylist.)

137

Always remove those thread belt loops on dresses and replace self-tie belts that may reveal how little you paid for an outfit. Adding a nice leather belt or changing to better-quality buttons can give a dress a more expensive look. When you buy an inexpensive outfit, make sure the hem is even all the way around, for it rarely is. It always makes me feel good to redo a hem with lace seam binding. It's almost like adding some pretty underwear to your outfit.

Organizing Try to arrange things in your closet so that everything can be seen.
Your Closet You should be able to walk in, look, and pull out what you want.

In dealing with a dark, undersized closet, the first thing to do is to get one of those little lights that works on a battery. Put it up and use it. You'll suddenly be able to see everything, instead of having to fumble in the dark.

Label everything clearly from the outside. That includes garment bags of clothing, as well as shoe boxes and hat boxes.

Store clothing that's out of season out of the closet, or on the back rung or the rung above. If there is room in your closet to build this extra rung, it's a good idea to have it done. It doubles your hanging space.

If anything can be visible, let it be. Plastic coverings over everything assure cleanliness, but they also limit closet creativity. You can even forget you have items when they're all under wraps.

Knits that will stretch out (double knits are usually sturdy enough to hang normally) should be folded in half and then folded again over a soft bar hanger—you can wrap the hanger with a wad of tissue paper so it won't mark the knit garment. By folding your knit, you halve the weight and therefore halve the stretch. Or knits can be folded in drawers, with tissue paper or cleaners' plastic bags between them. Just don't block a stimulating view of the variety and color of your garments.

Don't get into the dresser-drawer syndrome. We all had mothers or grandmothers who would receive a lovely gift and then promptly pack it away in the bottom drawer for some far distant occasion grand enough to justify wearing it. You live today. Wear your clothing and enjoy it. Nothing lying unworn in a dresser drawer can flatter you or make you feel terrific. And that's our whole goal, isn't it?

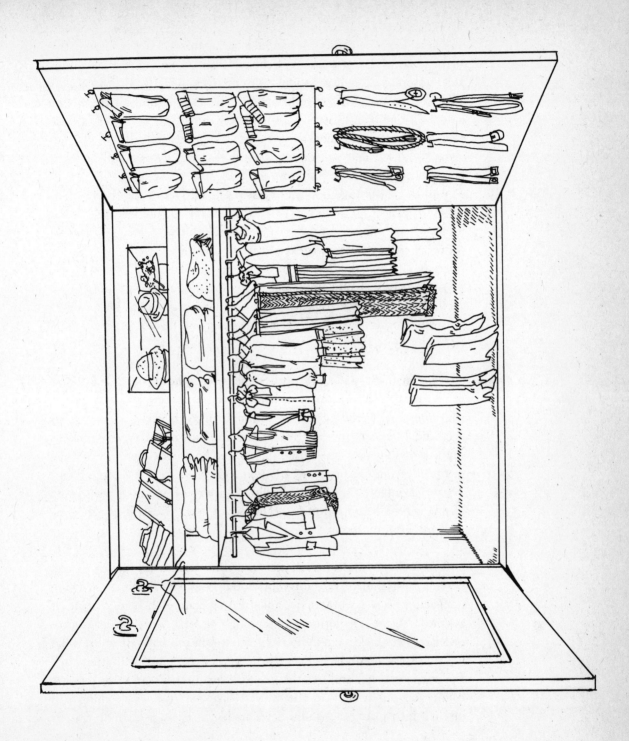

The clothes in your closet should be organized into categories that make it easy for you to see and choose what to wear. Everyday things, this season's, of course, should go up front. Hang all the jackets together, all the skirts together, all the pants together, all the dresses together. You should separate suit jackets from their skirts or pants, so you'll be sure to use them with other separates as well. If you've got a two-piece dress, and you can wear the top separately as another blouse, you probably won't do it if you don't see it hanging with the blouses. Put all the shirts together, the dressier separated from the sportier, and all third-layer tops together. All sweaters can be folded on a shelf, preferably on the shelf near your skirts and pants, so that you can see immediately if colors and textures work together.

Hang all the belts on one of those special belt hangers, so they can be seen easily and kept untangled. Bags should be lined up on a closet shelf. Try using shoe bags for hanging all your shoes in one place on the back of the closet door; then you can easily match shoes and bags and belts right there.

Developing a *Rhythm of Care* Maintenance sounds like a gruesome subject, doesn't it? One couple my husband and I know has a standard running joke about the basket of ironing and mending the wife brought into the marriage two years ago, and that her husband swears remains untouched to this day. At the risk of sounding like Pollyanna, let me point out that any task can be fun if you're not pressured and if you can look at it in the right way. That even includes sewing on buttons. I save all these little tasks to do during a good television movie. That way I end the evening with some sense of accomplishment.

Approach repairs and maintenance with calm and patience, and develop a rhythm of care for your clothing. Make a habit of checking items after you've worn them, and then separate each item that needs attention before it's worn again, sending the dress you spilled a spot of coffee on to the cleaners right away (while you can still remember what it was that caused the stain). Take the pair of pants with the stuck zipper to be fixed, and get the broken clasp to your necklace repaired before you put it back in the drawer. That way the whole thing will just fall into place, and you'll never find yourself in a clothing frazzle.

Never hang back in the closet anything that needs mending. It belongs on a separate hook. Team your clothing in a relay system. If Team A is at the cleaners, be sure that B is on deck and ready to go. There's nothing especially saintly about getting things done ahead of time—it's simply more sensible. And it doesn't take any longer; in fact, it's sure to *save* you time in the long run.

For some people, getting dressed means a dreadful business of hopping around on one foot looking for the other shoe, discovering a run in the last pair of pantyhose, suddenly noticing buttons missing right smack in the middle of your bosom, followed by a last-minute scorching on the ironing board and then a decision that the whole outfit was wrong, anyway.

That's not the ideal way to get dressed. Whenever it's humanly possible, especially if tomorrow's an important day, you should lay things out the night before. That means everything, including jewelry, belts, scarves and underwear. It's the only way to make dressing a pleasant experience and your clothing message clear and deliberate right from the beginning.

One good reason to lay things out is that most of us don't really have enough closet space, and our clothes are pretty much scrunched together. Given the chance, wrinkles might just hang out overnight or steam out in the shower the next morning, and you won't have to go through a major pressing operation.

In the morning, do your hair and makeup before you dress, so you won't get the clothes mussed and have to start all over again.

Protect your hair and makeup with a sheer chiffon scarf when you pull clothing over your head.

Then check yourself in the mirror at least once before you put on your coat, and once afterwards.

The whole routine shouldn't take more than thirty or forty minutes—and that's a forty minutes well worth investing. I'd rather set my alarm early and start the day feeling on top of the situation.

By now, your closet should be in order. You've hung everything back where it belongs; all strictly evening wear together, all outer wear, all third layers like jackets and vests together, all skirts together, all pants together, and so on. You've bagged the discarded stuff for the

*And Now
You're Ready*

141

Salvation Army, or set it aside for others. You know where you stand on the clothing that's in your possession, and you have an idea of the kind of basic wardrobe you want to own.

From now on, it's a matter of determining what else you need and setting out to get it.

*Consider
Your Life-Style* To budget properly, you must first understand your own needs and priorities. About how much of your time do you spend in office attire? How much in clothing for just running around, for entertaining or active sports? How many of your outfits must be multi-functional? How much of your life is spent as wife, mother, hostess, professional? And which is most important to you? You may spend more time in the office, but those occasional evenings at the theater may be the high point in your life, so it's all right for *you* to spend more for evening clothes. Women who work generally spend up to three quarters of their clothing budget on a wardrobe for their career, the rest on leisure or dress attire. Some work clothes double for dress wear, too, of course. In choosing your own priorities, take your personality and your preferences into account, and budget accordingly.

*You May Not
Need It at All* What you think you require, you may not need at all. The best way to determine your life-style needs is to keep track during a typical week of the number of times that you don different clothing. Perhaps five times a week you put on clothes for work, twice for social occasions, three times for sports, or carpooling or what have you.

Next, get a clear idea of the proper wardrobe for these activities. Does dinner out with your friends mean to them, and to you, a pants outfit or a cocktail dress? Do you feel comfortable wearing a long gown to the theater, or do you prefer a regular-length skirt and blouse?

I suggest to clients that, if it helps them, they post, on the inside of their closet door, the list I send them of all the possible combinations of their clothes. You can make such a list, too, so that when you're in a rush you'll have a quick guide to what works for you.

*Creating Your
Combinations* Go to your now organized closet and list the wearable items under the life-style categories that you've made. List each skirt, and, under it, each blouse or sweater that makes a flattering outfit on you. Then, if

it's needed to finish the look, list the third layer—a jacket or vest or outer shirt—in the left margin.

Example:

Green skirt

(green-tweed blazer)	a. cream-silk smocked blouse
(black-velvet jacket)	b. lavender-and-green flowerprint shirt
(green-tweed blazer)	c. white cowlneck sweater

You'll see what you're missing for a totally finished look; you'll see where, though you have a coordinated skirt and blouse, they are not important enough to be an ensemble—you're missing that third layer. (A truly distinctive blouse often doesn't need a third layer.) List pants the same way, list dresses with coats or jackets to cover, list long evening gowns with what goes over them, list long evening skirts with blouses and their cover-ups. As you list these things on paper, you'll be able to see right before your eyes where you've got only one color family in your whole wardrobe and it's dull, or where you've got all solids or where you have *no* totally finished outfits.

Next, write down the ideal number of additions you need to fill out each category. You may want to use colored inks to indicate different color families.

Figure out how much you can spend on your new commitment to yourself: which items should be bought first, which can wait and which can be sacrificed most easily by, perhaps, wearing clothes from another category. Keep in mind that everything new has to be integrated with your own present look. You don't want to have a bunch of old clothes with a few new ones sticking out like sore thumbs. You want a careful blend of clothing that will give you an effortless, individual, stylish appearance. This will happen automatically if you repeat this process every year.

Everyone has the right to express herself through clothing. Of all the clothing hang-ups women have, undoubtedly the most paralyzing is guilt. Many women feel they don't deserve to spend on themselves.

One client admitted she had to invest in psychoanalysis before she could make a commitment to spend on herself. Once she made the decision, it was a firm resolution to care for herself in the best possible way, and that doesn't mean spending foolishly. After all, look at the amount of homework I'm asking you to do before you spend a cent.

Another woman was unable to spend while she was heavy. She was ashamed of her body, and it wasn't until she had lost ten pounds that she was able to treat herself to a new dress.

If you live with a man and feel defensive about your burgeoning closet in contrast to his neat suits hanging in a row, forget it. Men, particularly in the upper-income brackets, tend to spend as much on clothing as women.

Sometimes a client feels she's worked out her guilt and is convinced it's okay to spend on herself. I notice that if we happen to find more than three items that are right for her in one store, she is simply unable to buy the fourth, even though we've not come close to her budget limit. At the next store it's okay, she can spend again—just not too much in one place. I have a few clients who never seem to "find the occasion" to wear their new purchases until the following year when they're safely "old clothes."

Restrained by guilt, many women buy too cheaply and sacrifice both their money and their image. Occasionally, a woman will finally outrun her guilt for a little while and, in the unreality of the moment, spend a good deal more money than she needs to.

I've found that it relieves guilt considerably if you select a firm budget figure each season, do your preplanning as we've discussed and then stick with that plan. Keep a record of what you spend, so that, as your wardrobe becomes fuller, more interesting and more versatile, you have proof that you did not overspend.

I realize there will be some of you who will have little, if anything, to spend on your wardrobe, so budgeting seems beside the point. If the rent's not paid, if Billy's outgrown his sneakers and has to have shoes for school, then obviously that's the financial priority. Even if you can't go out and spend on new clothing just now, the evalution of what you own and the inculcation of fresh ideas should still help you look better and project your clothing message in a more articulate and exciting way. Perhaps you can afford only a couple of scarves just now, but they'll lift your spirits and give a new look to some old outfits. You are taking control. With your new understanding, you are making maximum use of your present wardrobe. And that has to feel good.

It's the woman with the most limited budget who can least afford to make mistakes. If you're fearful of making errors, my advice would be to go against your natural instinct and blow this first season's budget on one core item important to your wardrobe; perhaps a well-tailored blazer basic enough to go over the old skirts and pants in your closet to make complete new outfits. Next year you'll see why that one purchase was a wise decision, because with your second year's budget you can buy two blouses, two sweaters and perhaps another skirt to go with that jacket. And on and on, each season adding to your core wardrobe a few quality clothes you really like.

The difficult part is the shifting of gears to start building a new wardrobe that isn't full of compromises. Once that first sparse season is over, you're on your way to having a good time with the language of clothing.

9
The Hunt

Shopping has been a passion, a pastime and a delight for me for as long as I can remember. I've always gone to stores with the same enthusiasm that others regularly visit theaters or art galleries. I used to spend every free moment enjoying my hobby. And I knew where all the best merchandise was in the city. I was bursting to tell others where the great coats for that season were, or to describe a fantastic belt I had found in some small, out-of-the-way shop. Even when I go abroad, while others are hitting the beaches or the museums, I head for the nearest "Five and Ten." It's my way of getting the pulse of a new country. I love to wander up and down the aisles, to see the gadgets and learn the different ways that people in other countries solve the prosaic problems of life—from the design of a shoe horn, to kitchen utensils, to baby clothes. And then I head for the little, local boutiques! I love it all!

Making a Disliked Task
More Difficult

I guess I may be different from many women, because so often I've heard "I don't think I could ever tell you how much I loathe to shop." Or "Shopping? I'd rather die!" For all too many, shopping is a torture second only to root-canal work, and, as one who loves it, I used to wonder why. I have one client who is a dynamo when speaking to large groups about the stock market, but get her to the entrance of Saks Fifth Avenue and she starts quaking in her boots. Other clients, reacting in various ways to the trauma of outfitting themselves, become unusually quiet, or helplessly gregarious, or teary, or nervous and negative, or judgmental and superior.

Barbara always used to leave shopping to the very last minute because that gave her the excuse to fail. "After all, how could I be expected to find the perfect outfit in such a short time?" Then if she did just "happen" to succeed, she could consider herself a heroine!

Another woman, who has a normally cheerful disposition, used to wear a look on her face, as she pulled each garment down over it like a shroud, that seemed to say she was carrying all the agonies of the world on her shoulders. Every time I attempted to help her pull down, blouse, zip up, or turn hems, she'd make an overadjusting body move-ment. It was her game that either I—or the clothing itself—was pushing her around. "You see what a pain it is to get myself together? You see how much hassle I have to go through?" That gave her the rationale for not having made the effort all her life. However, she loved the way she looked in the new wardrobe, came back the following season and now she no longer plays that game.

We all have our own ways of making a disliked task more difficult. One client tries too hard to hold her stomach in all day, and begins to hyperventilate; another, a thirty-five-year-old professional who had been too long in junior dresses, was in a state of exhaustion by noon on our first day out—because she was fighting the growing-up that each outfit made her confront. For her, maturing was a strenuous process.

Old patterns from the past still affect many people. I have one client for whom coats are an almost unbearable trauma. When she was a little girl, her mother made an enormous project out of coat buying and forced her to buy a coat at least two sizes too big, so she could "grow into it." Although she does beautifully with almost everything else in her wardrobe, she still has a terrible time buying coats.

The women who come to me for help are, on the whole, highly intelligent and accomplished people. Not only do they have the city of New York, one of the world's largest marketplaces, from which to choose their clothing, but usually they also have a budget adequate for what they need. Yet, when it comes to buying clothes, many just can't cope.

Risking Your Image and Your Money

It's easy to understand the strain that all women are under. There's a lot at stake when you set out to find your style. You're risking two very precious commodities—your image and your money. What you do may cause a big change in your life. When women have a problem with shopping, the culprit is probably fear, coupled with confusion, followed by frustration, followed by a blinding headache.

Sometimes it's a plethora of goods that's the problem—too much of a choice. The inability to make a decision can be agonizing. Sometimes the problem is just the opposite; there seems to be no choice.

The Fruitless Search

How often have I heard women wail, "I know what I want, but I just can't *find* it!" Perhaps you've had that experience. You see women on the street every day wearing the clothing you're just dying to have. When you go to buy it, it's suddenly nowhere to be seen. You become convinced that as soon as you walk into a store a silent alarm is sounded and all the *good* clothing is rushed into the back room.

I guess I don't need to point out that that kind of attitude is just a little paranoid; stores really *do* want to sell you clothing, and it's certainly to their advantage to stock what's in demand. *It's just a matter of knowing where and how to find it* and of avoiding the mental paralysis that sometimes takes over—so that even when you do see the item you want you don't recognize it.

The "Knock the Customer" Game

Also contributing to the shopper's anxiety is the "knock the customer" game played by all too many in the merchandising field. You may feel marvelous self-esteem at the office, but as soon as you walk into a fashionable store you have the distinct impression that you are unwelcome, unfashionable and undeserving. Now, this particular bit of "paranoia" is probably *not* imagined; sometimes the store employees *are* doing a number on you.

I was first exposed to the world of retail sales from the "other side of the counter" right after I got out of college, when I began one of the best jobs I could have had to launch my career in fashion—a work-study program on Bloomingdale's executive training squad. It was an exciting world, with customers like Paul Newman and Jacqueline Kennedy Onassis to wait on, but I also found that working in a pressured merchandising operation is a grueling experience. I developed eternally aching feet, which quickly grew from size 7½ to 8, and my hands and clothes were constantly filthy from moving stock around. I found my patience severely tested by dealing with people and problems that would challenge the diplomatic skills of Kissinger. I learned that the only common bond of most of the store team—buyers and sales help alike—is an antipathy they develop toward the customers. It's so easy to fall into the habit of gossiping about shoppers and to affect a haughty, "put down" manner. At least it serves to make the job a little more interesting and to maintain a sense of camaraderie among the employees.

I'm sure most retail-store employees begin by wanting to please, but because of the stress of the work, their early resolve quickly deteriorates into frustration, resentment and a cynical disregard for the customer's best interest. I wonder how many times in my years of shopping I have seen clerks, on commission for each sale they make, tell an uncertain customer that what she's trying on looks "absolutely wonderful." Unfortunately, this kind of false reassurance or intimidation works most of the time. The shopper accepts it and allows the saleslady to take control.

"It's Just Perfect for You"

Years ago, when I used to witness these scenes, I always wanted to go over and say, "No, it's absolutely wrong for you, *don't* buy it." I realized that it wasn't right to offer criticism, to tell the woman what not to buy, unless I was willing to help her find what she *should* buy. Perhaps that's really how the idea of my business was born, from seeing so many people who desperately needed a facilitator, someone to help them resist the pressure and clarify their confusion.

To counter the "knock-the-customer" game, first convince yourself that *stores are for looking just as much as they are for buying.* You are entitled to respect and courtesy without spending a dime for it. When people who are investing their time in shopping don't buy, it may be a fault in the store's selection, display or service. Even if the store is carrying terrific merchandise, it's okay to be "just looking" and getting inspiration. Don't be intimidated.

Often people think it's okay to browse a bit, and even try on a few things, but if they get into any kind of extended session, and realize it's not going well, they automatically begin to look through the items they've tried on to see which would make the least odious token purchase. There's no need to waste your money that way. You didn't manufacture all of that clothing that doesn't fit you. You didn't stock the store's shelves inadequately. You weren't the cause of their being out of size 10 in the only two items that interested you. Just thank the clerk. If she's been helpful, tell her so; say you'll be back again, and leave. Shopping can become a more pleasant experience when you realize that sales personnel are just as human and just as insecure as all the rest of us. They don't really *mean* to be nasty, and they probably won't be unless you allow it. By indicating that you understand their problems, you will help to establish a rapport which will help you and perhaps make the day a little more pleasant for the clerk.

Shopping requires careful planning and preparation, reconnaissance and strategy. It's called knowing the marketplace. Take the time to list on paper the most likely shops for the items you need. Take a little extra time to study the local ads in the newspaper. Letting "your fingers do the walking" is not such a bad idea. Also, go back through those fashion magazines you've been studying; compare them with the list you've made of new clothing you'd like to have to expand your existing wardrobe. As you've probably noticed, many of the ads list local department stores for the goods that they feature, but don't count on those stores actually having the items in stock. These ads are generally highly unreliable, because they must be ready for the printer about six months in advance; in the meantime, most anything could have gone wrong. First call the stores that advertise the items, but don't set your heart on something until you've got it in your hands. Magazine ads are inspirational. Newspaper ads are more accurate for actually determining where to find a particular garment.

If you're getting a runaround when you're trying to find something that you know the store carries, because you've seen it in a front-window display or a store advertisement, try calling the publicity department. Their whole reason for being is to get you to respond. So they'll respond to you.

Another excellent way to know your marketplace, and to obtain a little higher education in the language of clothing, is to attend the fashion shows provided free by many of the larger stores. They're often both an eye-opener and a valuable, painless lesson. When I was working for *Seventeen,* I was sent on the road to do commentary for fashion shows all over the country. The fashion show is a happening to be experienced. In it, you see an outfit totally pulled together by professionals. The clothing is "performed" for you in a theatrical way, occasionally with real eloquence.

Every store caters to a particular kind of customer. The stores do, of course, overlap in some merchandise, but the selections are often quite different—its presentation and the emphasis that give each store its special ambiance. Whenever you have a chance, drop into a store you haven't visited before. It probably won't take more than ten or fifteen minutes to learn its personality. You can quickly see which stores you want to add to your regular shopping route, and you can eliminate certain stores and boutiques as not having anything for you. Keep checking new stores as they open and old stores as they change their styles, so you'll be up-to-date as to where you can shop.

The Store for You (And for the Occasion)

Consider how well each store suits you and your personal style. What is its general image, its level of taste and standard of service? Is the store exciting to you? Are you comfortable in its atmosphere? Is the lighting pleasant or dismal? Do you like the sales people? Do the clothes fit you well? (Some boutiques have their own "fit" which caters to their clientele.) Are the prices in line with your budget?

Some women prefer stores with better-trained sales people, home-delivery and pick-up service, charge accounts and gift wrapping. These privileges add to the pleasure of shopping, but they also add to the cost of the purchase. Other, more stalwart, souls feel right at home in stores that have fewer sales people, larger crowds and offer less services, but reduce prices accordingly. It's up to you—where do you feel comfortable?

Remember, you can buy at both kinds of stores. That way you can, for instance, take advantage of the style sense of an expensive store for an elegant item, but also benefit from the less expensive store's prices for more basic garments. Buy your black evening pants at Macy's because of their tremendous selection and price range, but purchase the silk evening blouse at a Bendel's or a Neiman-Marcus. If you need an important accessory, like a fantastic print shawl to update an old outfit, do go to the more fashionable store to take advantage of its buyer's eye for the latest chic.

If an item is not currently in fashion, you will be frustrated if you try to find it at the most fashionable stores. They don't carry items that aren't "in." But you may find a good selection at a store that specializes in the basics. I learned my lesson trying to find sweater dickies in the wrong year.

If you're shopping for a special occasion, and you know that the uniqueness of your dress or costume will be judged, don't try to buy that dress at your standard department store. For some women, indulging in one small item from a specialty store (any store, larger than a boutique and more exclusive than a department store, that caters to the whole woman) makes them feel more "turned out" than a whole new outfit from Gimbels.

There's nothing more rewarding, after you've played the shopping game for a while, than buying a bargain at a middle-price outlet and wearing it out of its usual context. People will exclaim that you must have gotten it abroad or in some mysterious, unknown boutique. Then you really feel you've beaten the system.

The Scouting Trip   If there are more than two or three outfits on the list of planned additions to your wardrobe, and if you're at all uncertain about your ability to keep your wits when you're shopping, then it's probably a good idea to do research for yourself on a day before you actually purchase, just as I do for my clients.

Group geographically the stores you intend to visit. Make some phone calls, and then, on your research day, start off armed with nothing but a pad and pencil. There is a marvelous feeling of freedom when you know that you're not there to buy. With the attitude of a researcher, just mark down prices, styles and sizes available.

When you approach stores with this businesslike attitude, I think you'll be surprised at how little hassle you'll get. Clerks will realize quickly you're not going to buy today, so they won't hover like vultures. They might whisper amongst themselves, but you're no longer intimidated by that. You might explain to a friendly clerk that you're doing research for your big purchase day, and she may even offer to lay some clothing away for you, as they always do for me, now.

On your research day, you are pulling together looks that work for you. You're concerned with balancing the potential new purchases with looks you already have in your closet. You're checking for proportion in outfits, seeing if they're scaled to your body. You're working with colors and prints, coordinating tops with bottoms, and with accessories. You're deciding how your budget should be spent, which pant or skirt should perhaps be eliminated because you can't find the right blouse to complete the outfit. Also, most important, now that you know what you want your clothing message to be, you're analyzing each ensemble to determine whether it speaks your message.

This is the time to experiment with that new line you're curious about. Since it takes several exposures for the eye to adjust to a new hemline or a new shape, it might be wise to try on a couple of items in that new look, even though it's only your research day (most of the try-ons can wait till later). Some of us tend to like what's current right away, but for others the new styles take some getting used to.

On your research day, do notice how the other shoppers are dressed what the sales clerks and other people on the street are wearing. Remember to take it easy and keep your mission in perspective. Don't feel you have to go through every rack on display, or look at every single item available. Stick to your list. You could, of course, miss the buy of the century, but it's unlikely. And realize that you don't have to make a single decision all day!

At this point, you may be saying to yourself, "Well, that all sounds very nice for people who have the time to do it, but when you work five days a week, it's a little difficult to take an extra day just for scouting." I'm sure it is. However, you're making an investment in clothing that may involve a week's pay or more. It makes sense to take a few extra hours to do it right. Go at night to research; the stores are open late just for people like you.

Years ago department stores were just that; they used to be arranged in very easily recognized and clearly defined departments, each selling its own specific category of clothing. Nowadays there are so many more

Finding the
Right Department

options—and that can be exciting. It's up to you to be familiar with the territory.

On your research day, check out the various departments. You may have had the experience of asking a store manager where to find a wool skirt, and having her rattle off the names of six departments—Town and Country, Contempora, Individualist, City Slickers, New Riviera. . . . All these tell you virtually nothing about the style, size, or price of clothing to be found there. Dividing the department store into small boutiques is today's merchandising theme, designed to encourage and stimulate—almost force—customers to wander around the store.

On a scouting trip, you can reconnoiter six departments in fifteen minutes. It will become clear very quickly which departments are best for you. Also check out different departments for special items. You may not want to shop in the Elegant Sportswear department regularly, but that may be just the place to find the special vest or belt you need to complete your new skirt-and-blouse ensemble.

Save Money on Hidden Treasures   If you are lucky, you may be able to pick up a sexy evening gown in the Loungewear department, a great sundress in the Swimwear department or a fun loose peasant dress in the Junior Dress department. Even when you're not a Junior in age any more, Junior dresses and coats can be a good bet if they fit your figure and if you choose an ageless style like a classic trench coat. If maillots, one-piece bathing suits, are in, and your figure is in shape, buy a dancer's halter leotard, which costs much less than a maillot in the Bathing Suit department. A cotton, open-work shawl from the Beachwear department may be much less expensive and go just as well with that evening gown as a silk shawl from the Eveningwear department. The Men's department may be a good source for some purchases, too. Men's casual pants are sometimes a good buy, especially a good-quality wool-gabardine or tweed trouser. It's incredible the way they resist wrinkles; the fabric is terrific. Be sure, however, that it's a cut flattering to your female form. Don't forget that Men's departments give free alterations!

Get good deals by buying off-season. A Columbus Day coat sale can often save you a bundle, and robes and nightgowns, as well as many other items, are usually very attractively priced after Christmas; August is good for summer clearance sales. Think ahead and plan ahead. Don't *buy* too far ahead though—styles change, and you change, too. Remember me and my wedding dress!

Boutiques

Back in the 1950s, most American clothing was mass-produced. But in the sixties, all of that changed with the advent of the boutique, which provided a sort of way station between custom made clothing and full-scale manufacturing. A new unknown designer could, with a modest investment, produce a relatively small number of garments for a boutique clientele. And if the style caught on, both he (or she) and the fashion could become an overnight success. It was a wonderful opportunity for young designers to get started without a lot of capital.

The word boutique simply means shop in French. Although, when the movement first started in this country, boutique was a fairly special kind of shop, it's now come to mean just about any clothing store (or department within a department store) that is not very large. Boutiques can range from tiny, magical places with handmade goods to those strobe-lit dens with earsplitting disco music. Some of these boutiques are so heavy on atmosphere and hard rock that the last thing you could possibly think about is buying a dress. Others are charming, and some are exhilarating and exciting.

Shopping in an uncrowded boutique can be an absolutely fearful experience. There may be three coffee-drinking salesladies waiting to pounce, to festoon and bedeck you and then punch it all up on the cash register. Or, on the other hand, they may be so comfortable with their gossip and coffee-sipping that they seem to resent your intrusion and glare at you malevolently. In the best boutiques, you can have the advantage of chatty, personal contact with the salespeople, or maybe even with the owner. The merchandise is limited, because of limited cash outlay and limited space for stock. Every sale counts, so they usually want to do their very best to make you happy. And boutiques often have a very distinct, individual style, so when you find one that suits you, you can keep coming back for more. Boutique shopping can be particularly pleasant for the repeat customer as the store personnel comes to know her taste.

The Spree

On the day that you do the actual shopping, there's more preparation involved than just remembering the checkbook and credit cards

155

and trudging off with an empty shopping bag. You should go about planning for this trip in an organized way.

First, consider what you're going to wear, and remember that comfortable, low-heeled shoes are an absolute necessity. Also, take along the shoes suitable to the outfits you'll be trying on. Faking it by standing on tiptoe doesn't give a true picture.

Your clothing message for the day should be cool, self-contained and reasonably solvent, but not ostentatious. Plan on being a quick-change artist. Wear a front-zippered, one-piece dress, if you can, and underwear that won't shame you. (You've already picked out that all-important, well-fitting bra.)

A zippered tote bag that your purse will fit in is a good means of carrying all your supplies and belongings. Always keep your purse in the bag, make sure the bag is closed and keep it, not just in sight, but within grabbing reach. Picked pockets and purse snatchings are not the way to improve your attitude toward shopping! If you don't have the store's charge plate, carry traveler's checks and identification with you rather than a large sum of cash. I have a friend who landed from abroad with $600 in cash in her purse and then lost every cent of it when, unwisely, she took it shopping with her. Also carry with you all the information you need—the name of the store manager who gave you information about an item over the phone, clippings of the design you're looking for, the name of the manufacturer whose pants always fit you well and, of course, the notes you made on your scouting trip. Remember, you'll be less susceptible to sales pressure if you're already fortified with the facts on what you want.

If you plan to match clothing that you have at home, if you want just the right color or type of blouse to go with a specific skirt or if you want to buy a longer length raincoat for your new-length dresses, bring the item along. Avoid spending energy explaining or describing to some sales clerk who likely won't know what in the world you're chattering about. By having the items with you, you'll reduce doubt and eliminate return trips to the store. If the garment is too bulky or clumsy to carry, maybe you should wear it.

Expending Energy in the Wrong Direction   Take care to fix your hair and put on the right makeup. It will make a big morale difference in front of those heartless mirrors. Some of my clients are so distracted by their disappointing appearance that they spend all day apologizing about how they look. That's energy expended in the wrong direction.

It's important to make this shopping trip alone. Family and friends can stay at home and cheer your purchases later. You're learning your own style, and so you need this opportunity to contemplate your choices alone. At this vulnerable stage, a friend might be just too influential. It would be terrific if she could be there for support, but the risk is great that she will just confuse you.

Family and Friends Can Stay at Home

You should plan to arrive at the store when it opens. The money you invest is likely to go a lot further if you're not crowded or pushed or harassed. There is as much as an hour of absolute blissful calm in a store before business really gets going. And the sales help is at their best at this time.

As soon as you get into the store, go right to the checkroom and check your coat and extra packages. Yes, it's true, although many people don't know it, there is a checkroom in almost every large department store, usually on the ground floor. It's more than a convenience; it's a blessing not to have to drag around heavy coats and umbrellas and other encumbrances.

Now, with your list before you and your outer garments safely stowed, you're organized and ready to begin.

In blocking out your shopping trip, plan to hunt for the most important and most difficult parts of the outfit first. For example, if you want a very special print top to wear with pants, first look for the more difficult-to-find blouse, and then match it with the solid-color pant. (Of course, if you have a hard time fitting pants, look for them first, then find the blouse to match.)

Where to Hunt First

If boots or shoes are on your list, it's a good idea to try them on early in the day, before your feet start to hurt or swell. Coats seem to be a difficult item for many of us, so try them on when you're fresh and have energy, either first thing in the morning or right after lunch.

You should go directly to the first department that sells the main items on your list. Don't get distracted or waylaid by the clever displays

Insidious Budget Breakers

that have been set up to impede your progress. As you move through the store, keep your resolve firmly in hand. The pressures to buy are enormous.

One of the most fascinating things I've learned about retailing is how, just by showing merchandise differently, you can make it sell. It may be the same old stock, but, with a clever display, it comes alive and people buy, whether or not they had any intention to do so when they entered the store. Beware of these insidious budget breakers. Remember that a large percentage of the profits in department stores is made on impulse purchases. It's all part of the presentation; on a body it's called illusion, in a store it's called merchandising.

Now that I've warned you about enticements, let me say that impulse buying is different from just chancing to see an item that you've been looking for, or know that you will be looking for in the near future. If you don't buy it when you see it, it may not be there when you come back. If those comfortable shoes that you'll need for next month's vacation suddenly come into view as you're riding up on the escalator, go ahead and take advantage of the unexpected find. It will be the very item that will elude you when you go out specifically to look for it.

"Staying on Top"   I've learned in my business that when I'm in a store I must "stay on top." Make a conscious effort to maintain your concentration and equilibrium. When the elevator door opens, don't daydream; be there consciously all the time, and you'll never have that scrambling-to-keep-up sensation.

One cause of department-store headaches is that you're looking at too many things at once. When you push through crowds, seeing a hundred faces, it becomes totally exhausting. I avoid focusing on other people's eyes when I'm on a shopping expedition. I try to keep my sights on my immediate goal. In a situation where there are such tremendous and artfully contrived stimuli, concentration can help to keep you from getting dizzy.

When you enter a department, don't allow sales people to take you over. Look around first and get acquainted with the merchandise. Don't accept help until you're ready for it. It's perfectly okay to say, "I'll let you know when I'm ready." Of course, if you visited the store previously on your research trip, you may already be known.

It's perfectly okay to change sales clerks. No one owns you just because they got to you first. If you happen to get stuck with a "booster" who vows that every item you try on is just perfect for you, it would be wise to change to someone else. In this situation, loyalty is misplaced. Simply say you'd rather look around for a while, and then find yourself some more helpful help. Let the salesladies fight it out between themselves after you've left.

Prices and Inflation

I've always thought it odd that women's clothing is priced in definite steps. For shirts in a top quality department store, the prices seem to be $24, $45 or $60. The pants run $45, $65 or $95. I don't know the reason for this. I suppose it's to take advantage of people's ingrained habits. If you customarily wear $45 pants, you're not confused by looking at the other price groupings.

Of course, men still get the best deals on clothing. Men's clothing is almost invariably made better, the detailing is finer and the manufacturers don't seem to cut as many corners.

A fine cotton man's shirt costs about $25. A really fine woman's cotton shirt costs twice as much. Why is that? Because fashion has a more important influence on the women's clothing market and the cost of designing, fabricating and merchandising women's constantly changing garments is higher. But as glamour, fad and changing fashion begin influencing the male clothing market more, rising costs will inevitably drive the prices of men's clothing up, also. And then, gradually, men will become willing to pay higher prices, too. It's only a matter of time.

How to Tell Quality

The whole construction of a garment can be approached from a number of economic points of view. A blazer that sells for say, $50, may require perhaps thirty-five steps in its manufacture. A $100 blazer may take sixty-eight operations, or a hundred and ten. The difference is usually quite apparent.

Inspect a garment to see that it is constructed properly. Investigate the seams to be sure that they aren't puckered. Check that the zippers lie flat and that they have the strength and durability you'll need for that garment. Make sure skirt linings are fitted a little more closely than the outside skirt, to take the strain from the outer fabric. If the fabric has a pattern, stripes or plaid, they should be matched along the seam lines and pockets. If clothing is not cut on the bias, then lengthwise threads should generally be perpendicular, and crosswise threads should be parallel to the floor.

A fairly easy way to get some lessons in quality tailoring is to spend time in the men's department of a good store. Take ten minutes to examine the inside of an $80 suit, and then check a $300 suit the same way. You'll see the difference immediately.

When you make a conscious decision to sacrifice quality for some other feature that you want, you should know what you're giving up. One thing may be the life of the garment—it may hold up only until the first dry cleaning. Or you may find yourself sitting down to the sewing machine, reinforcing splitting seams the very first week you own that bargain.

Sometimes it's okay to buy inexpensively because the item is faddish and you don't expect it to last too long. Such items may last a little longer if you dry clean them. Do buy an inexpensive garment loose enough so that the seams won't be strained and split. Keep in mind that the quality of the tailoring is more obvious in a solid-colored garment.

When you buy inexpensive clothing, you may blunt, or even destroy, the clothing message that you have worked so hard to achieve. Recently I was walking up a New York street behind two young women. I never did see their faces, but I learned a lot about them, anyway. Both had shoulder-length hair. Both wore trench coats, which they had belted behind them so that the coats were open and flying in the breeze. Both wore pants, both carried shoulder bags of canvas and the two were clearly friends. But that's where the similarity ended. The brunette was wearing an authentic trench coat made of good, heavy, khaki cotton, beautifully tailored with definition, presence and style. Her slim, black, well-cut trousers hung perfectly, so that one could see just the proper half-inch of her patent heel. The safari bag slung on her shoulder was canvas with leather trim, and she walked with the energy of a confident woman.

The other woman wore a coat made of too thin a cotton in too light a shade. It was a flimsy covering that had lost its shape at the cleaners.

Her pant leg hung badly and showed too much of a wrong shoe, a straw espadrille in the fall. Her shoulder bag was a sagging, soiled canvas affair that lacked the dash of the other girl's. Both young women had invested time, thought, money and energy, but only one's clothing image was an asset.

"Can you believe it?" the woman exulted, pirouetting in front of her husband. "I'm a size 8 in these pants!" But is she really? You may have had the experience yourself—you normally wear a 10 in off-the-rack clothing and a 12 in foreign imports, but in designer pants you're suddenly a sylph-like 8, and you haven't lost a pound! American manufacturers of higher-priced clothing make a conscious effort to please the ego with their generous sizing policies. Women are far more likely to invest in a size 6 than they are in a 10, and cheaper clothing does tend to be cut somewhat smaller.

Unraveling the Size Mystery

A tale that I am told is not apocryphal involved a cutter who discovered he could get more garments out of less material if he first crumpled up the paper pattern that was supplied to him and then smoothed it out again. The crumpling had the effect of making the pattern shrink uniformly, perhaps a quarter of a size. The manufacturer he was cutting for never knew the difference, and at the end of the week the cutter had several bolts of material left over, which he then sold to someone else. It's corner-cutting like this that makes "cheap" clothing cheap. Judge your true size by medium-priced wear. In less expensive garments, you will generally be one size larger; in higher-priced clothing, you will be able to slip nicely into one size smaller.

Since my occupation depends upon having a finely developed eye for clothing, I don't need to try on every garment anymore. I know a few other women who can take a chance when they're in a hurry, but I'd say that generally it's a tricky business and an unnecessary gamble. The agony of try-ons comes only when you're not prepared or dressed for them. It can all be done quite painlessly, and remember, every time you try on an article of clothing is a learning experience.

Every Try-On Is a Learning Experience

First, you pick out the garments that you want to try. If you have a question about size, carry both sizes into the fitting room. If you're not allowed to take in as many articles as you want, just ask the clerk to hold them for you.

161

I always carry that sheer scarf we talked about in Chapter 7 for my clients to tie over their hair and face before they put a garment over their head. It saves wear and tear on both makeup and hair. It also saves face in another way—you won't incur the wrath of the store personnel in the event of an accidental lipstick stain. Since pulling things over your head won't be a struggle, you'll be apt to try more things on.

A lot of women tell me they feel they lose most of their looks and all of their dignity the moment they step into a fitting room. I try to assure them that everyone's skin looks mottled under that harsh fluorescent light, and that most people feel dumpy when they confront themselves in their underwear in that mirror. It can be a rather depressing experience—a reminder of that second helping of cake that you shouldn't have had, or of the broken resolutions about taking care of your skin or buying yourself some pretty underwear. Also, some women are annoyed by the sales people who always seem to poke their heads in at just the wrong moment—when they're in an awkward position, struggling to get something on or off. If this bothers you, just tell the clerk quite firmly you'd rather be left alone until you call her.

If you're trying on an important garment, you should put the whole look together in front of the mirror. I fix and fuss just as if I were getting dressed at home, in order to see if the garment is really for me. Relax and take your time; that's what a dressing room is for. Then look at yourself objectively, and try to imagine the impression you would make walking into a room wearing that garment. One free moment, remember? Is it the impression you want to make? Do you feel the way you want to feel?

Try sitting down in the dress or skirt or pants. Try scrunching the fabric in your hand to see if it wrinkles too easily. Try anything else you want to—bending over, reaching out, doing a deep knee bend. Does the garment do all the things you'll want it to do when you're actually wearing it? Can you move in it? Be sure, for instance, that the armhole of a garment is set where your arm socket is. If the armhole is too low, it has a web effect and holds your arm immobile.

If you're not sure of how you move in an outfit, or how you and the outfit move together, go out on the selling floor and walk around in it. But be careful about those inevitable compliments from saleswomen on the floor. The unspoken response from other customers on how you look will provide a more accurate barometer. If any garment that you're trying on needs tugging or hauling or constant adjustment, forget it. Remember that an uncooperative dress will never look good or make you feel good.

Before making any kind of final decision, be sure to check labels to see what kind of cleaning or washing care is needed. Are you going to be willing to do what is necessary? Also take into account possible problems with shrinkage.

For the clerk who's urging you to let her wrap up a garment right away, when you haven't made up your mind or have already decided that the outfit is not for you, here are a few good, stock replies which may help to get you disentangled:

"The dress is beautiful, I just don't feel good in it."

Or, look her calmly in the eye and say, "No, thank you."

Or, "Let me think about it. You were very helpful and I'll come to see you again."

Whatever you say, it's your tone of voice that's going to get the message across.

When you feel your decision-making power is getting a little fuzzy, now is probably the time for a break. Heed those first little warning signs. If your feet are tired, or you're getting a twitch, get out of it for a while. Have a cool, invigorating drink (preferably non-alcoholic—you need a clear head for shopping) and some kind of healthy, protein snack. Take the time to regroup, and check your purchases against the budget you prepared. You've estimated x dollars for x number of items, and things might not be turning out quite the way you'd planned. The vital figure is the overall one, however; you will tend to go over on some and find ways to save on others. That is okay, just as long as you stay within your total budget.

Resisting the Hard Sell

In the flush of the moment, you may very well pick out one white elephant. So, before you make any final decisions, clarify for yourself once again just how the garment demonstrates new clothing language skills and articulates your new image. Does it introduce a new color or shape or mood? Is it special enough, or do you already have something

Mistakes

like it that will achieve the same purpose? Finally, is the purpose it achieves worth the price of the garment?

If, after all this self-searching, you do make a mistake, and can't return it, don't feel too bad about it. We're all entitled to a few, and I think that these experimental purchases also serve a necessary function. They give us new perspective and sometimes a start in a new direction. You may go too far, particularly at first, in trying to achieve a new look. A mistake is probably the quickest way to learn what you can or cannot carry off.

Some shoppers never can seem to make up their minds. They prefer to shop and try on all day, then attempt to remember which part or piece they liked in which store, and go back to buy. I think that's an energy-wasting approach. Right or wrong, you should make decisions as you go. Traipsing from one store to another and then back again to "try on that first dress just one more time," eventually has a stupefying effect. The decision you finally make will be based more on fatigue and confusion than on your own good taste. Gradually you'll come to trust your first instincts more. You don't have to spend your entire life shopping—even *I* don't think it's *that* much fun!

Alterations   The principles that apply to altering garments at home also apply to alterations in the store; generally size changes are practical, but don't attempt to alter the garment for style. Hems can go up or down, hips and bust and waist can be changed. Shoulders can be tricky.

Don't be misled by the optimism of the alterations lady in the store. She has a vested interest. She'll be pretty honest as to the technical sewing problems, but she won't be able to say for sure what the alteration will finally look like, and whether it will be worth the trouble and money to you. Remember, alterations alter a little; they don't magically transform. If you're not sure, maybe it's better to look for another garment.

Store Conveniences   Charge cards can be the greatest! Just those magic words, "Charge and send, please," can turn shopping from drudgery to delight. In many reliable stores, you don't even have to wait while the sales slip is written up, so long as you know the clerk's name and they know the "send" address. You can sail out of a department and on to your next purchase without even waiting for the paperwork to be finished. Do write down the number of the sales check before you leave, or get that send receipt (which I ask for before my saleslady spends the time filling out the whole sales check).

By the way, clerks, like other people, just plain enjoy being addressed by name. I've heard complaints from salesladies that some customers, whom they have known for years, never bother to ask their names, even though the clerk may know the customer's name, address, size and style preferences—and even her children's and grandchildren's names. Treat the clerks as you'd like to be treated if you worked there. It's not only polite, it usually pays off in better service.

Most department stores will not only deliver merchandise, particularly for a charge account, but they'll pick it up for a small fee if it's to be returned. Take advantage of that service, too. Be sure to have someone at home to collect a receipt of pick-up. Otherwise, you're sunk if the store says they don't have any record of it.

We've all read about celebrities who call up and have "a few dresses" sent over to try on. This is a service that's available to more than just those privileged few. Through the use of charge accounts and the store's own shopping service, many women do take advantage of this opportunity if they feel more sure of garments tried on in the familiar atmosphere of their own home. Of course, wearing a garment and then returning it is definitely unethical. Return policies are often phenomenally generous, so don't misuse the privilege.

What about the No Exchange/No Return policy in some stores? In some cases, it's not totally inflexible. You probably still have a chance for a return or exchange even after the store's time limit has expired. If you have a good case, try it; at least it's better than just throwing out faulty merchandise unused. Your best bet, if you're willing to take the time, is to go to top management. They usually try to be accommodating.

Other store services you can use include summer storage of furs (furs are usually cleaned, stored safely and insured) and repair departments for handbags and shoes that require special care. If you have a favorite department store you find yourself at home in, take the time to investigate services they offer that make your life easier. Stores ought to put out an easy-to-read brochure, like those you find in hotel rooms, detailing all of this.

Remember that clerks or department managers can often find out for you when shipments are expected to come in; this may be totally new merchandise or replacements for stock already sold. (You might ask them to call you when it arrives.) That way you don't have to settle for a sweater that's one size too small if a new shipment is coming in the following week. You can sometimes "special order" merchandise in a size or color that's not in stock. It may take a few days, or even weeks, and, of course, there's always a slight risk in buying a garment you haven't actually seen. But when that dress is just the style you want, and they don't have that perfect blue in your size, special ordering might help you get just what you are looking for. Remember to take the manager's name, so you can check periodically to see if your order is in, rather than having to tell your story each time you call.

What Stores Ought to Offer

Wow! The thought of designing a store just for the convenience and comfort of the customer—I'd like to do that some day.

One improvement I can think of right away is to install more flattering lighting. If you had a dimmer switch in the dressing room, you could change the mood. Under a harsh glare, it's not easy to imagine what a dress will look like in a dimly lit restaurant. (Of course, if that dress looks halfway decent under the deadly cold fluorescent light of most fitting rooms, it will look dynamite in better light.)

I think it would also be nice if department stores offered free alterations for women; that would be true equality, since they've always done it for men.

There ought to be restrooms on every floor in big stores, not just one or two for the whole place. It would also be great to have some nice comfortable chairs placed around the store, near coffee stations.

Soon it will be possible to go to almost any store, big or small, with just one bank credit card and have money transferred directly from your account, without writing checks or carrying different cards for a dozen different stores. So you can spend more money with less effort!

But all of that is for the future. As of now, things are the way they are, and we deal with what's out there. For you, if all's gone well, the shopping trip is happily concluded. You're at home already, with your feet up and a cool drink in your hand. With your trophies all stowed away in your closet, you're ready to start wearing your new look and merging with your new image.

10
Integrating Clothing and You: An Ever-Evolving Image

Wearing with style the clothes that do the most for you and make you feel your best may not instantly confer health, happiness, security and love, but the way that you're now putting it all together should tell others that you care about feeling good—and that, after all, is the point of looking good.

You're an Original, a Walking Work of Art

Every time you step out of your door, you are a walking work of art, an original. It is careful daily tuning, matching and planning of your wardrobe that makes the critical difference in how people perceive that work of art. Some women, who've resolved to improve, psych themselves up to the point of buying new clothing, but then they let it drop right there; they never follow through—and they miss the most creative part of all. If your new outer image does not merge with your *self* image it remains a shell, something which you don and doff, and it will be apparent to others that it's just a surface thing—an exterior decoration.

Immediately after making a new purchase, while you're still excited by its newness, integrate it into your wardrobe. Spend some time in

Integrating New Clothing

front of the mirror, mixing and matching it with your other clothing to make as many new and *improved* outfits as you can. Have your makeup on, your hair combed and wear the right shoes. Check your accessories for those that suit the various combinations, and make a list of anything else you may need. This try-on session at home is always my favorite part of a shopping expedition, for it's when I really lay claim to my new purchases.

Whenever you invest in a new and different fashion look, for heaven's sake, take it home and *practice* it. Sit, stand, walk. Coordinate the garment with your body. Integrate it into your own mannerisms—learn to move with it. It's worth a bit of practice to avoid stumbling or strangling yourself.

A friend of mine was once invited to a gala theater opening which the president and his wife were attending. She took exquisite care in preparing for the occasion, buying a new gown and a long, elaborate evening cape. She arrived at the theater with her escort in a shiny Mercedes. As the car pulled up, she was evidently mistaken by the crowd for a big-name celebrity, and there was a round of cheers and applause. A bit flustered, she stepped out of the car—and right onto the edge of that unfamiliar long cape! She nearly fell over on her face. Needless to say, she has practiced with each new garment ever since.

The Key to Chic Is Appropriateness The key to chic is appropriateness. If everyone else is in formal wear and you show up in stunning sports attire, that's not very smart—and probably not very considerate. You lacked sensitivity to the situation and didn't use your common sense. It's possible for your dress to be individual and still appropriate.

Don't Overwhelm Don't ever seek to overwhelm the world with your clothes. Dress down when it's important not to antagonize or frighten people, or set up competition. Always keep in mind who you are, who your audience is going to be and what you want to project to that audience. If you're going to your husband's partner's house for dinner, if you know that there've been difficulties between the two of them recently, and you also know that his wife just isn't your match in style, then surely the last thing you want to do is make a strong, competitive fashion statement that would only further divide the two camps.

On the other hand, it's sometimes important to let your clothing speak money or power quite loudly. Many people dress down when they visit their doctor or lawyer, on the theory that if you look as if you have any money at all you'll be overcharged. Actually, I think it's far more likely that you will receive better treatment and service from almost anyone if you look as though you have some status.

Also, when you go to the hairdresser's for a new hairstyle, it's really foolish not to arrive with your hair—and clothing—already looking good. By looking good you'll challenge the stylist to create something even better for you. Go with the ironies of human nature—everyone likes associating with a winner.

He likes you *au naturel,* when your hair is loose and flowing and you're wearing no makeup. Perhaps you feel at your worst that way. Your best bet is to be sensitive to his wants in some regard—to make some compromise or concession that you feel you can live with.

Keep in mind that, while self-expression is fine and should take first place on your list, if you dress *only* for yourself you're going to be left out of the ball game. It is very possible to dress for your man, for men in general, and for your career—all without slighting any aspect of yourself.

When I was first married, I realized that my husband really wanted me to dress in pale tweeds and cashmere—to be a kind of all-American girl with a Candice Bergen look. That, obviously, just wasn't me. But I made some concessions wherever I could, without sacrificing my identity. Gradually I convinced him that I was right about not imitating Candice. Now he's proud of me in my own style, and has forgotten all about hoping I'd become the image that he'd grown up to think was his ideal.

If the man in your life wants you to look "sexy" and that's just not you, perhaps he'll settle for your looking stunning, with attention-getting clothes that are in good taste but not provocative. Or, if your job calls for strict dress and you tend to be flamboyant, how about satisfying those needs with a few fantasy clothes for evening? Or some really important jewelry to enliven the prim attire that your boss insists on.

If your clothing tastes are quite sophisticated but your job calls for frequent travel to a small town where you stick out like a sore thumb, should you compromise on the issue? I think you should. It's easy to alienate by being overdressed. If you wear simple, good clothing, your out-of-town associates will still recognize the quality, but they'll appreciate your softer-spoken statement.

<table>
<tr><td>

*The All-Important
Job Interview*

</td><td>

One of the questions I'm most frequently asked is what to wear to that all-important job interview. The answer is to remember one simple, basic rule: dress as though you already worked there.

</td></tr>
</table>

If the company is casual, a soft silk blouse and skirt is a good choice. If you discover the company is more formal, and suits are *de rigueur,* of course wear your best tailored two-piece. But keep in mind that a lot of executives may have trouble with a super chic female decked out in a hat and a Halston suit. You might do better with something a little less elegant and unfamiliar. Choose an outfit with impeccable details, particularly those that will be seen from the waist up. This includes your collar, your jewelry, your cuffs and, of course, your makeup and your hair.

<table>
<tr><td>

*The Right Place
to Dress
Is at Home*

</td><td>

Dressing is something that you do at home, not when you're on the move all day long. It's not attractive to be pulling and hauling at your clothes in public, so take the time to do it right in the morning. Tie and wrap carefully, so you won't have to adjust constantly. Straighten bows, pull down blouses and then lift your arms for that comfortable looking blouson ease. (Blouses will sometimes stay in place better through the day if you anchor them under the waistband of your panty hose.)

</td></tr>
</table>

Actresses and models, whose beauty is their profession, may spend an hour and a half getting dressed in the morning—but then they forget about it. You never see a confident woman primping, or touching her hair or face; most even try hard never to be caught looking in a mirror. The carefree and unselfconscious look is a very large component of graceful beauty.

<table>
<tr><td>

*Helping the
Weather Out*

</td><td>

Plan for the psychological effects of the weather. It's amazing what a bright-red, happy dress can do for a rainy day. At dreary times in your life, playact at being in a better mood by using color—even colors that

</td></tr>
</table>

are new for you. Some people seem to want the natural, protective colors of dull grays on a gray day, but you can reverse the trend and brighten your mood and the mood of everyone else around you.

No one looks quite as ridiculous as a woman all dolled up in an elegant, dark suit with dark stockings on an unseasonably hot spring day. Girls are blooming all over downtown streets in summer dresses, while she trudges along in the heat with beads of sweat on her brow. Conversely, there's nothing more pitiful looking than the wilted flower after a hailstorm, shivering in thin, pink voile.

This may sound like your mother talking, but check what the weather will be before you plan your outfit for the day. It'll save embarrassment, misery and ruined good clothes and shoes.

If you'd like to be remembered, or if you want the product you're selling to be remembered, wear something unforgettable—some color that's particularly unusual or attractive on you—or an important, attention-seeking accessory, such as an unusual belt, a pendant, an old watch or a beautiful pair of earrings. Integrate the item into your wardrobe and let it be a conversation starter. There is an automatic transfer of feelings from a person to an object she may be identified with—and vice versa. If we see a woman modeling a dress or standing beside a car display, what we feel about that woman influences how we feel about the dress or the car. That is why people in sales particularly must be constantly aware of their dress. *Memorable Dressing*

I said a little earlier that clothing must be appropriate, and that appropriateness is inherent in the definition of chic, but now I'm going to say that it's okay to contradict that rule sometimes—in the right way. For example, fabrics and colors are usually determined by season. But white (or off-white), which is thought of as a summer color and an evening-wear color, becomes "drop-dead stunning" when worn in the winter during the day, provided that it's translated to wool. A number of young designers are making use of this effect—velvet for sportswear, cotton muslin for evening peasant blouses and the illusion of evening sheer fabric for day wear. Appropriate in this case means appropriate for you: can you carry it off? *Breaking the Rules*

Use tasteful rule-breaking when you wish to stand out just a bit more, when your mood or situation demands that you be more readily defined and noticed.

*Don't Look
Too Perfect*

There are times when one shouldn't look too perfectly pulled together. It's kind of refreshing to see a bare neck and ears on someone who's always adorned with jewelry. Sometimes a strapless sundress or evening gown becomes you, and has a sexier look, because your skin is totally bare—there's just *you* there, glowing and looking wonderful.

Sometimes those perfect little earrings are not quite perfect; they can also make you look uptight, not casual or carefree enough. A flower by your ear might do the trick better. It will all depend on your mood, and the crowd you'll be with.

*The Image
That Bombs*

Always keep in mind that a too carefully put-together look can easily become a contrived look—the image that bombs. In any creative endeavor, when you can read the thoughts of the person who put it together, there's something wrong. You may have had this experience when, while watching a film, the mechanics of plot and production became so obvious that all illusion was lost. I'm sure you've also walked into a house that's been so carefully decorated it has become a showplace and not a home.

Sometimes clothes steal the scene in a way that's no good. The scarf that blows in your face as you walk down the street, the collar or lapel that flares up into your face and smudges your lipgloss, the wrap skirt that unwraps itself at the wrong moment—they make you look awkward and feel foolish. A little care and practice ahead of time can prevent these mishaps.

Also, beware of your own unconscious mannerism that may detract from an attractive appearance. Fidgeting with your hair, pulling at your skirt or collar, these cancel the very best effect. Only the nervousness comes across. Try to see yourself objectively; such habits can be easily eliminated, so that your clothing message will come through loud and clear.

*The Six-Months
Checkup*

There's probably no more worthwhile investment of your time than spending fifteen minutes once every six months in self-evalution. Check out your body objectively, just as you've done earlier in this book.

172

Sometimes it changes, and you don't even notice. Study yourself once in a while in a store mirror, preferably a three-way mirror in the privacy of a dressing room. And take a second long look at some candid photos of yourself. See if you're getting a little dull or a little lazy. Or, on the other hand, are you taking your new image too far? Ease up; it's not true that more is better. Getting yourself a new look is good; exaggerating it is not.

When there's a red-letter day in your future, decide what you're going to wear ahead of time, rehearse it all once, check it out, then put it away and forget it. People often become so conditioned to worry about what they're going to wear that often they groan even as they're taking the invitation out of the mailbox. An invitation is supposed to represent an opportunity to have a good time. People don't send them to you to punish you or to put you through the wringer.

Dressing for
Important Events

Not long ago I was invited to participate in a large and glittering charity event at the Plaza Hotel in New York. It was a very busy time in my life, and I just put off thinking about what to wear. I was so sure there must be something in *my* closet that would be suitable. By procrastinating, I very nearly blew the whole thing. The weather that day was unexpectedly hot, and the only suitable evening gown I had was a long-sleeved, high-necked one, which would have been ridiculous and very uncomfortable. Luckily, I managed to dig out a white halter gown that could get by. It wasn't particularly impressive, but, by adding a special, fancy hairdo, done hurriedly by a wonderful friend, and a single fresh flower in my hair, I managed at least to look cool and reasonably attractive. If I'd been wise enough to follow my own advice, I'd have checked the weather forecast, looked in my closet and had a chance to pull together an outfit that would have been as special as the occasion warranted. And I could have arrived feeling calm, instead of frantic and rushed.

That trip you're looking forward to is a special event you should plan ahead for, too. Take along only those things that you *know* will work for you. The experienced traveler never packs something which has just been hanging in her closet. If she hasn't worn it at home, chances are she won't wear it on the trip, either. She knows which hem length of which skirt goes under which coat, and she knows what heel height is right—which shoes are most comfortable for all the walking that's needed. She knows that one or two sets of accessories will take care of every occasion. And she knows that all the garments she chooses fit comfortably and will pack well. On a trip you want to have fun, not worry about your clothes.

Disasters   How about when you've done everything you can; you've planned and prepared for a special event, and then at the last minute something terrible goes wrong—a rip, a spot, a hem suddenly giving way. It's okay; stay cool. There's no need to let things throw you. Your inner self-image will carry the outer image through these emergencies. Besides, no one's going to observe as acutely as you think they are, unless you yourself are thrown by the disaster.

I remember one fashion show when I was doing the commentary. Just before I had to go out on stage, the zipper down the back of my dress gave way. So I had to go on, wearing a very obviously pinned-up dress. I willed my attention away from it, and concentrated on the show. It worked! Nobody even noticed it, because I relaxed.

If you haven't got the right clothes you need for an event and you can't get them, do the best you can and let others' comments fall where they may.

"Dressing Well   Diana Vreeland, former fashion editor of *Harper's Bazaar* and *Vogue*
Is a Habit"   Magazine, once said that dressing well is a habit. You must dress well every day, or you're not going to be able to pull off a success on that one special evening. In the coming months and years, as you continue to evolve and refine your own unique style, dressing creatively will become an ingrained habit. Always remember that taste is not the same as style. Taste involves caution; style demands courage. Although they are corollary traits, to have taste is not necessarily to have style. Style is your personal aura, made visible.

A New Era   If you had been absent from the planet for twenty years, wouldn't
of Style   you be surprised by all of the changes in dress that have taken place? For both men and women, clothing is now more expressive, less regimented and confining. More and more, we're speaking out about what we want to wear and what we don't want to wear. We women

have the power to reject restricting stereotypes of beauty. Fashion will, and should, continue to change with the times, but we no longer need accept constantly changing and capricious designers' designations of the so-called ideal woman.

With women becoming themselves, with standards of beauty becoming more realistic, perhaps the present idealization of youth will give way to an acceptance of the natural process of aging. As medical experts realize that some of the qualities we've associated with age are actually symptoms of poor health, we're beginning to realize that the aging person can be attractive and graceful, that she can be physically, mentally and sexually active by taking care of her body as well as her head. Women over forty probably look better now than ever before in history.

As women take control of their own bodies, as they grow healthier and more certain of themselves, there's less need for camouflage. Fabrics are sheer and lighter, and heavy undergarments are gone. Clothing is now designed to describe the natural body beneath it. We are emerging from an age of strictly observed fashion into a new era of personal, individual style. And we are the first women ever free to express, through clothing, not merely our class, profession, wealth and sex—but ourselves. Past ages of enlightenment have not included women. This one *centers* around us.

The personal style that you're now learning to express through your clothing can extend into every area of your life—your work, your home, your taste in music, the way you enrich your life or relate to others, right down to the simplest acts of wrapping a gift, writing a letter or planting a garden. Whatever you are doing, do it with style, and let that style be *yours*.

(SEE FOLLOWING PAGE FOR COUPON.)

Start Looking Terrific Now

...with an individual wardrobe plan, worked out especially for you, via computer, by Emily Cho herself!

Here's your chance—thanks to the computer—to get from this leading fashion authority and consultant some of the expert help and guidance that has brought her hundreds of clients. And it's all yours for only $24.95.

Send in the coupon below, and you'll get a wide-ranging, comprehensive questionnaire, filled with the same kind of probing questions Miss Cho uses in her private consultations. You'll enjoy filling it in—indeed, just thinking about the answers may give you a better idea of the dimensions of your wardrobe problems.

You will then receive a written report—complete with clothing illustrations—relevant to your own personality, body, and lifestyle needs. It will show you how to disguise your body faults and enhance your assets. How to stop making clothing mistakes that cost you dear in money wasted and self-confidence undermined. How to put your best You—your *real* You—forward. Not just now and then, but every day. An Emily Cho wardrobe is designed to *work.* That's why it's not an indulgence—it well may be the wisest investment you'll make this year.

Miss Emily Cho
Emily Cho, Inc.
P.O. Box 1594
Cathedral Station
New York, NY 10025

Dear Miss Cho:
I want to start looking terrific now. Please send me your questionnaire for my individually planned wardrobe. I look forward to receiving my illustrated written report within 5 weeks after I return the completed questionnaire to you.

Enclosed is my check for $24.95. (Please add $2.00 for additional postage and handling outside the continental USA.)

Name _____
(Please print)

Street and No. _____

City _____ State _____ Zip _____

(This coupon may be mailed anytime after September 1, 1979.)